PHOTOWORKS

Photography, Art, Visual Culture

Issue 21:

Collaboration

Become a Photoworks Member

Photoworks Membership includes
Photoworks Annual (RRP £20) shipped direct to your door
Access to Members-only web articles
10% year-round Photoworks online shop discount
Seasonal exclusive offers
Priority booking for Photoworks events
VIP and preview invitations
Brighton Photo Biennial launch invite

UK Membership £25
International Membership £35

Photoworks is a registered charity, join Photoworks today
and you'll directly support our programme and help
us to champion new perspectives on photography

www.photoworks.org.uk/members

photoworks

Photoworks and the editors would like to correct the error on p. 196 and pp. 202 - 204 where the following works have been incorrectly captioned.

The correct captions are as follows:

p. 196. Andrew Lacon, Studio Sculpture, 2014. Steel & Velvet
p. 202. Andrew Lacon, *Reference Works No. 12,* 2013. Painted Steel
p. 203. Andrew Lacon, *Agalmatophilia: Fig. 1,* 2013. Painted Aluminium
p. 204. Andrew Lacon, Reproduction of Sculpture, 2014. Framed Photocopy

Photoworks would like to apologise to the artists for the editorial oversight.

This issue of *Photoworks Annu*
collaboration and photography
from Brighton Photo Biennial a
of the Annual accompanies.

Entitled 'Communities, Co
BPB14 consists of nineteen exh
of new commissions based on i
collaborations. Photographers l
communities, marine biologist:
community groups and with or
bodies of work. Curators, edito:
have come together to generate
on different archives. Curated e
existing modes of collaborative
ular focus on photography colle
of *Photoworks Annual* showcase
the Biennial, much of it previou
lished. The projects are accomp
further exploring the issues rai:

The theme of the Biennial r
inence of collaborative modes of production, dissemination and reception encountered across areas of
photography in recent years. Writing last year, Daniel
Palmer identified a 'collaborative turn' in contemporary art photography, as artists involve the public
in the production and dissemination of work. Some
timely interventions in the theorisation of photography

voices from anthropology, design, science, politics,
critical theory, new media, photographic history and
fine art together. We have also tried to provide collaborations taking place in our current moment with a
sense of those that came before.

Ben Burbridge and Celia Davies

Contents

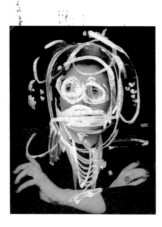

CONTENTS

BRIGHTON
PHOTO
BIENNIAL
2014

COMMUNITIES
COLLECTIVES &
COLLABORATION

4 OCTOBER – 2 NOVEMBER 2014

#BPB14   BPB.ORG.UK   @PHOTOWORKS_UK

BPB IS A PHOTOWORKS PRODUCTION

Contributors

ABC (Artists' Books Cooperative): international group of artists who create, engage and communicate on issues relating to self-publishing through book fairs, exhibitions and the online forum abcoop.tumblr.com.

Geraldine Alexander: currently researching Fay Godwin's photographic archive.

Mariama Attah: programme curator at Photoworks.

Juliet Baillie: researcher on amateur photographers and camera clubs in the 1930s.

Daniel C. Blight: writer, art critic and curator, and blog editor at the photographersgalleryblog.org.uk.

Ben Burbridge: co-editor of *Photoworks Annual* and co-director of the Centre for the Visual at the University of Sussex.

Burn My Eye: international photography collective of street photographers who share their work on burnmyeye.org.

Federica Chiocchetti: writer and independent curator, and founder and director of the photo-literary platform photocaptionist.com.

Celia Davies: director of Photoworks and co-editor of *Photoworks Annual.*

Matt Daw: projects manager at PhotoVoice.

TJ Demos: writer on modern and contemporary art and photography and reader in art history at UCL.

Liam Devlin: writer and lecturer whose research explores documentary imagery in relation to socially and politically engaged art practices.

Andrew Dewdney: involved in community photography since the 1970s, now lecturer in the Department of Arts & Media, London South Bank University.

Brian Dillon: UK editor of *Cabinet* magazine, and reader in critical writing at the Royal College of Art.

Eugenie Dolberg: photographer who has worked extensively in the Middle East producing the book *Open Shutters Iraq* (2010).

Elizabeth Edwards: visual and historical anthropologist interested in the relationships between photography, anthropology and history.

Jason Evans: photographer and lecturer, and founder of thedailynice.com.

Simon Faithfull: contemporary artist whose practice includes video, digital drawing, installation and writing.

John Fleetwood: head of the Market Photo Workshop – a school, gallery and project space in Johannesburg, South Africa

Nick Galvin: photographic archivist, lecturer and information specialist, and former archive director of Magnum Photos, London

Haidy Geismar: writer and researcher interested in culture, property rights and the digital, and lecturer in digital anthropology at material culture at UCL.

Roger Hargreaves: writer and curator at the Archive of Modern Conflict.

Jan von Holleben: German photographer whose work has been exhibited internationally and published widely throughout the world.

Max Kozloff: art critic, art historian, photographer and recipient of the International Centre of Photography's Infinity Award for Writing.

Kalpesh Lathigra: photographer and recipient of the W. Eugene Smith Fellowship and Churchill Fellowship.

Caroline Lucas: Green Party MP for Brighton Pavilion and a former Green Party leader.

Anthony Luvera: photographer, writer and educator who has exhibited widely in galleries, public spaces and festivals.

David Alan Mellor: curator and writer, and professor of art history at the University of Sussex.

Christopher Morton: curator and anthropologist interested in the relationship between photography and anthropology.

Christopher Pinney: anthropologist and art historian, and professor of anthropology and visual culture at University College London.

Annebella Pollen: researcher and writer interested in the history of mass photography, and lecturer in the history of art at the University of Brighton.

Kerry William Purcell: writer on graphic design and visual culture, and lecturer in design history at the University of Hertfordshire.

RUIDO Photo: a network of photographers, journalists and designers exploring documentary photography as a tool for reflection and social transformation.

Aaron Schuman: photographer, writer, editor and curator, and founder and editor of the online photography journal See-Saw Magazine.

Erica Scourti: artist and writer whose work in text, video and performance has been shown across a range of international institutions, galleries and festivals.

Thabiso Sekgala: South African photographer whose work has been exhibited internationally and explores themes of abandonment and memory.

Katrina Sluis: artist, writer, curator and educator, and presently curator (digital programmes) at The Photographers' Gallery, London.

Sputnik Photos: international collective founded in 2006 by award-winning documentary photographers from Central and Eastern Europe.

Noni Stacey: currently researching community photography in the 1970s.

Jennifer Tucker: specialist in the history of science, technology and Victorian visual culture, and professor of history at Wesleyan University.

Uncertain States: artist-led project that organises monthly talks and hold annual exhibitions publishes, and engages with the public by distributing a free quarterly broadsheet.

Jonathan P Watts: writer and critic, and lecturer in critical practice in photography at Nottingham Trent University.

Singular Images

CHRISTOPHER
PINNEY

JASON
EVANS

K. WILLIAM
PURCELL

MAX
KOZLOFF

LIAM
DEVLIN

protégez l'enfant !

A Sudanese Skirmish

Christopher Pinney

Behold a full-plate albumen print titled *Tirailleurs Soudaniennes*—Sudanese 'skirmishers', 'sharpshooters' or light infantry. It is a collaboration between at least six people. Five of them are staring at the camera and the sixth, Hippolyte Arnoux, a French photographer best known for his work on the construction of the Suez Canal, is behind the camera.

The viewer can immediately see the labour involved in producing this image, the logistical investments, and the complex performative contingencies that lay the material foundations for this 'representation'. In the foreground there is a redoubt made of what looks like the bark of cork trees—conveniently light, transportable and easily arranged in various configurations. In the background there are two different backdrops: a smaller one, which appears to have some kind of door in it, placed in front of some Arcadian scene. This features what looks like a European oak tree of the kind under which Gainsborough's Mr and Mrs Andrews might have sat.

Examine the poses of Arnoux's subjects—his 'skirmishers'. Some appear to be 'off message', and provide enduring testimony to the contingency of photographic collaboration. Perhaps it was their first time in front of the camera. The standing figures on the left and centre appear transfixed by Arnoux's apparatus and presence. The spear-wielding figure, second from right, certainly seems to have understood what we might imagine Arnoux's injunction to have been: 'Act fiercely! Threaten the camera, and hence the viewer!'

Arnoux's aesthetic and political project seems simple to reconstruct: an Orientalising vision of 'savage' others, easily realised in the imagination, but subject to quite different practical constraints photographically. Arnoux's image seems to perfectly exemplify Benjamin's wonderful observation that:

> No matter how artful the photographer, no matter how carefully posed his subject, the beholder feels an irresistible urge to search such a picture for the tiny spark of contingency, of the here and now, with which reality has (so to speak) seared the subject, to find the inconspicuous spot where in the immediacy of that long-forgotten moment the future nests so eloquently we, looking back, may rediscover it.[1]

Arnoux has pushed his artfulness to the limit, has carefully tried to pose his subjects to act out his fantasy of what they ought to be. But, because photography is 'seared' with the real, it is the trace of an event, it is always a happening or performance that depends upon collaboration, it will always be fissured by contingency. This contingency is rendered highly visible in this image.

If the photograph presents an intimate space—the collaborative claustrophobia of the studio—it also prefigures a very different encounter that would occur shortly afterwards in the Sudan. Arnoux was active between the 1860s and 1890s, and it seems reasonable to date this image to about 1880.[2] The term *tirailleurs* was first used to refer to 'skirmishers' who fought in advance of Napoleon's main columns, and subsequently served as a term for French colonial light infantry. Although the French formed *tirailleur* regiments in several parts of north Africa, in the Nile region conflicts with the British and the Ottomans prevented the consolidation of French colonial rule (after the Fashoda incident in 1899 the French would cede their claims to the Anglo-Egyptian Sudan).

This helps us to understand why these *tirailleurs* have only spears and shields, and to grasp the metaphorical and derogatory sense in which Arnoux may have been using the term. It also alerts us to a world-historical event in which these partly unwilling collaborators may well have been subsequently forced to collaborate. At the time that Arnoux probably made his image, Muhammad Ahmad, a messianic Samaniyya leader who proclaimed himself the 'Mahdi', led a successful revolt against Ottoman rule. Initially armed only with spears and swords, his followers, the Ansari, captured a large quantity of Egyptian rifles in 1883 and eventually conquered Khartoum in 1885.

The Mahdi's successor, Abdullah al-Taashi, would be defeated 13 years later at the Battle of Omdurman, which Sven Lindqvist suggests inaugurated a new epoch of death at a distance.[3] British artillery and maxim guns made possible the mass slaughtering of the lightly armed Ansari ('a matter of machinery' as the young Winston Churchill, who was there, termed it). Although popular accounts and images presented it as a hand-to-hand struggle, none of the Ansari got within 300 yards of British lines. It is generally agreed that in excess of 20,000 Ansari and only 48 British troops were killed. Kitchener, the British commander, called this a 'good dusting'. For Lindqvist, this actualised Conrad's premonition in his 1896 novel *An Outcast of the Islands* of the 'invisible whites [dealing] death from afar'.

Arnoux's photograph predates this world-transforming event that set the stage for a 20th-century marked by long-distance death. Arnoux's image, his trace of an event in the studio, is characterised by a closeness and intimacy with its puzzled collaborators. But it also presents us with 'the immediacy of that long-forgotten moment [in which] the future nests so eloquently that we, looking back, may rediscover it'.

1   Walter Benjamin, 'Little history of photography', in *Walter Benjamin: Selected Writings*, vol. 1, part 1, *1927–1930*, trans. Rodney Livingstone et al. (Cambridge, MA: Harvard University Press, 1999), p. 510.

2   Getty Research Institute, 'Union list of artist names full record display. ID: 500036539: Arnoux, Hippolyte. www.getty.edu (17 June 2014).

3   Sven Lindqvist, *Exterminate All the Brutes* (London: *Granta*, 1997).

A to B can be more rewarding when you end up at X. Imagine if Google Maps had a WTF function, and instead of routing you past Starbucks to your scheduled destination you ended up somewhere you didn't know you needed to be ... *need* vs *want*. A reoccurring dilemma for the digital cocoon snoozers. You might have to think for yourself, worse still have an unmediated experience. Off. The. Chain.

$$X + Y = ?$$

... another binary formula with multi-potential. *The Third Mind* by William S. Burroughs and Brion Gysin presents collaborations with cut-up techniques to facilitate 'disastrous success'. These new-sense, non-sense pieces are designed to reroute traditional understanding or undermine empirical power structures with associations that can require a leap of faith from the reader. A major drawback of the safe streaming of digital experience is the decreased potential for such happy accidents and insight-garnering mistakes. Throwing the Xs and Ys into the pot can be the catalyst for invention and discovery, and the creative selection of those ingredients depends very much on the open mind, of rejecting known formal conceits. Relinquish to receive.

Occasionally, red-eye drooling through Tumblr we can find such free associations. *This* next to *that* can propose hitherto unimagined couplings, and, while one man's mash-up is another's cacophony, these hybrids might signpost a way out of the current cannibalistic reference culture. Where print magazines would be used to offer provocative collaged juxtapositions (see Martha Rosler's *House Beautiful: Bringing the War Home*), we are more likely to establish such conflations in the de-contextual spaces of social media. The casual repositioning of selfies as soft porn alongside less fleshy consumables inadvertently presents a concise vector of our spiritual alienation. This is the flip side of the X + Y = ? argument ... total de-contextualisation creates the blandest soup ever. Without historical awareness, political positioning, authorial acknowledgement, original texture and all the other factors that make cultural artefacts the nuanced, resonant totems they should be, we will drown in meaningless mishmash.

Peter Fischli and David Weiss, *Untitled*, 1997–98,
Inkjet print, 29 ¹/₈ × 42 ¹/₈ inches. © Peter Fischli and the
estate of David Weiss. Courtesy of the Matthew Marks Gallery

The X + Y we are concerned with here is that of Swiss artist collaborators Peter Fischli and David Weiss, who worked together from 1979 until Weiss's untimely death in 2012. Their output is a mind-boggling range of formats and media that revels in process and the inclusive gesture of 'the reveal'. Irreverent and generous at the same time, they made at least two significant bodies of photographic work, each quite different to the other. *Sichtbare Welt* (*Visible World*) from 1997 is a survey of the known/seen, photographs that look like photographs of a world that we expect to see. The other work remains untitled and messes with that idea of photographic representation using deceptively simple double exposures. Just as the implication of artist-collaborators undermines the lofty value of authorship, this work creeps up on you with pretty colours and unassuming subject matter to deliver something cunningly thoughtful. Are we to imagine that Fischli made one exposure and Weiss the other? Why and how do these subject-images share the frame? Most importantly perhaps, what has been made? The melding of time, space and nature(s) proposes something else. All the time our brains are trying to unravel the two components, a denial of what is in front of us.

As an installation, cheap and cheerful prints covered the gallery walls in a psychedelic jungle, while projections pushed the montage further still. As one slide slowly dissolves into the next, we perceive four images simultaneously, or is that two? Complex visual formalism called into question so simply. The catalogue produced for the 1999 show at the Musée d'Art Moderne in Paris adds yet another line of enquiry to the proceedings. Loose leafed, unnumbered and ready to be shuffled, the publication is a series of folded posters, or single-sheet sculpture perhaps, as the paper's weight and crease allows them to stand confidently on the table. The folds' directions create further montages to complement that of the projections whereby we turn the pages to find two picture halves butted up together, and then sometimes no image at all.

There seems to be no let up in the revived fortunes of the photobook yet, whilst wading through a sea of grey, linen-covered wannabes, this flimsy volume resounds with an understated sophistication still relevant 15 years later.

protégez l'enfant !

Joseph Müller-Brockmann, 'Mind that child', 1953.
Photograph by E. A. Heiniger. Image courtesy of Museum für Gestaltung Zürich

Josef Müller-Brockmann and E. A. Heininger: 'Mind that child', 1953

K. William Purcell

The extraordinary development of graphic design as a potent means of communication owes much of its influence to the photograph. During the opening years of the 20th century, the photographic image remained formally distinct from the text it supported, whether in magazine layouts, adverts or posters. Yet, as the pace and intensity of the information environment developed through the early years of the 20th century, this polarisation of type and image was reversed. Technology initially allowed for the increasing enlargement of images, then the distinction entirely dissolved, when the idea of the photograph as a self-contained object was challenged by a series of pioneers who developed the graphic potential of the camera for a range of ground-breaking works. With a new visual awareness, such designer-photographers as László Moholy-Nagy and El Lissitzky exploited the graphic qualities of the photograph in works that aspired towards a formal synthesis across all the elements of a design. The resulting compositions circumvented the traditional idea of the photo as objective fact, a *trompe l'oeil* window on the world, in favour of an imaginative development of image and text. The outcome was a new approach to commercial art that transformed our modern visual language and helped to give birth to the figure of the graphic designer.

While many of the original applications of photography in design emerged from the aesthetic innovations of radical political change in the 1920s and 1930s, the desire for constant novelty and exclusivity within advertising led to the appropriation of many of the ideas for the sale of commodities. In fact, most of the original proponents of photo-graphics actively worked on both commercial and political projects simultaneously. Automobile advertising proved an important subject in these terms. During the 1920s and 1930s, the automobile stood as the visual motif of the modern age. Le Corbusier, for example, advocated the automobile as one of the leading illustrations of how the aesthetics of design achieved most success when surrendering to function. Modern designers were clearly attracted to this progressive image, and, as such, the motorcar became a recurring motif within posters of these decades and beyond. This seemed to be particularly the case in Switzerland, where the automobile was repeatedly represented as a sleek, potent and elegant symbol of modernity in a variety of works. Yet, this triumphant imagery often sat uncomfortably with the reality of a high death toll due to irresponsible driving. As a counterpoint to the homage to the car seen in Swiss graphic design, there is a tradition in Swiss poster design of civic campaigns alerting the public to the hazards of reckless driving.

Established in 1904, the Automobile Club of Switzerland (ACS) was one organisation that sought to address this issue. While promoting the liberating benefits of the car, in 1952 the ACS ran a competition for a poster design that would encourage road sense in drivers, cyclists and pedestrians. Seeing the call for the submissions, the Swiss graphic designer Josef Müller-Brockmann set to composing a design. He recounted in his autobiography *Mein Leben* (1994) how his opening effort picturing a child dangerously caught between two approaching vehicles failed to satisfy him. Continuing to work on it, Müller-Brockmann decided to eliminate the two cars in favour of a motorcycle. He envisioned it speeding along a road, bearing down on a child unaware of the impending accident. Yet, he was faced with the difficulty of how to realise an impression of a fast-moving bike without it becoming so blurred that the object would dissolve beyond all recognition. For this he looked to the skills of the Swiss photographer and filmmaker E. A. Heininger.

Heininger replied by photographing the front wheel of a motorcycle. He then achieved the sense of velocity Müller-Brockmann desired by positioning the wheel at a slight angle, so it appeared to be gathering speed. This impression of velocity was further amplified by a second exposure, in which he masked part of the wheel and then moved the image, generating a trail of light from the bike's suspension and wheel trim. In the finished design, Müller-Brockmann has positioned this image as an enlarged threatening presence, dominating two-thirds of the poster. A child (actually taken from a photograph of a child in a school playground) has been added, much smaller than the motorcycle, to create a sense of perspective, and seems destined to be knocked over by the onward-rushing bike. The vivid yellow 'road' at the bottom of the poster serves to heighten the sense of urgency. The black body of the bike offers a natural backdrop from which the poster's title, reversed out in white Akzidenz Grotesk type, reads 'Mind that child!'

The poster received first prize in the ACS competition. Heininger left Europe to work in the Hollywood film industry but, for Müller-Brockmann, it marked the beginning of a long and creative relationship with ACS, for which he went on to produce some of the most iconic posters of the 20th century.

Touches of the Unforeseen
Max Kozloff

When the subjects of a photograph collaborate with the photographer, their joint efforts, though often well registered, might still raise questions. The most utilitarian approaches to collaboration tend to be the most elementary, for they depend on the apparent spatial position and the social stance of the parties concerned. Usually, people are arranged or they arrange themselves—frontally—to demonstrate that they were 'there', constituents of an occasion. They might willingly have comported themselves on behalf of the photographer's interest, but for reasons of their own and for the sake of the image, which commemorates their particular moment of togetherness. They assumed that the camera, for its part, would be operated in recognition of their need to look good—or at least proper enough—for the reference of future viewers. Very well, but where to go from there?

I have in mind the commissioned portrait, whether of a single person or particularly a group. Each category within this genre has its own decorum, enacted by manners legible to contemporary audiences. Photographers may have been expected to coach the proceedings in order to serve up a modest product, for which they were paid upon delivery. In vernacular portrait studios and news magazines, in tourist areas, in glamour or fashion zones, in civic archives, in wedding shots, these commercial terms hold sway. The one who took the picture enjoyed only a temporary command of the affair, was generally an outsider to its community, and had modest status.

By way of contrast, think of a collaborative art that offers a rough parallel, the one governed by orchestra conductors. In proportion to their eminence in the field, they are respected for their many tyrannies over their designated groups. Individual players read from a score but are channelled as an ensemble by their leader, the master reader, in issues of pace, dynamics, texture and rhythm. Instruments produce the sound, while musicianship, from all hands and minds, collectively shapes its outcome.

No such prowess is called for from sitters, who are merely required to face a machine that goes no further than to record their appearance. They are non-professionals represented in a media service, which gives them a routine and passing attention. Other than its necessary

presence, there is nothing about their assumed pose that demands any artistry or theatrical skill (fashion models possibly excepted). The members of an orchestra perform for an audience that came there to hear them. The figures in a group portrait carry on in the limbo of their own ceremony, of whose outer circumstance we may or may not be offered a substantial hint.

All of which is to say—and no surprise—that a commissioned group portrait, like all photographs, exists as a fragment, a part of a story, at least as far as the narrative limitations of the frame are acknowledged. In this inconclusive assembly, the characters are nominally encouraged to lever out their differences. Certainly they are bonded for the nonce by their aggregate purpose, but who is to deny that they are also human beings, reacting in subtle latitudes of impatience or forbearance? What is expected of them is the look of team spirit or good will, sprung from their improvised cohesion. Yet, what is interesting in their display, other than sociological data, is anything amended beyond or beneath the requisite uniformity of behaviour.

Let me illustrate this thesis by a group portrait that remains socially articulate and psychologically explicit, even as it seems to break the rules of its genre. I will go further and say that it pulls out many of its genre stops.

Malick Sidibé was a photographer of the flourishing youth culture during the 1960s in his hometown, Bamako, the capital of Mali. His subjects were coming of age shortly after their African country had declared its independence from France and was finding its way in a post-colonial atmosphere. Memories of the tribal and traditional mores around him were preserved in the patterned backdrops of his studio and the starchy poses of elders in their village robes. The master photographer of that society was Sidibé's great predecessor Seydou Keita. Now, however, more urban vibes throbbed through the club scene of modish youngsters. They posed with their motorcycles, sashayed in bikinis at the beach, wore bell-bottom pants and danced away the night. Bangles and watches they conspicuously flaunted. Sunglasses and rep ties were very à la mode. The liberationist mood was enchanted by Western consumer culture and inspired by the voices of Jimmy Hendrix and James Brown.

Malick Sidibé made himself the pictorial laureate of this historical epoch. He speaks of his studio as the meeting place of a shifting crowd out for a lark, where 'I liked surprising people with their eyes closed, and… in weird positions.'[1] The fun to be had, immersed in their capers, he visualised in prints exhibited in his shop, ready for order. 'I always told people not to look at me', but despite his injunctions they often held antic, staring, hammy poses, as if to oblige their picture man. >

Malick Sidibé, *Family Party*, 1966.
Image courtesy of Malick Sidibé/Magnin-A

> Consider the image Sidibé calls *Family Party* (1966). In idiom, it resembles scores of his other frames where the gyres of celebration, as subject, and the need for descriptive control, as form, are kept in tense balance. A discreetly used flash adjusted to slow shutter speeds (1/8th of a second) accounts for his precision in locating figures wherever their rhythm carried them. It was important for him to catch them doing their thing, even if it distracted him from portrait focus. So, a reporter's overlook infiltrated his studio or 'composition work', where at times the two modes were indistinguishable from each other. To put it a different way: one gets the impression that some of the people included in the scene were not conscious sitters, and did not think of themselves as under observation. In that din, replete with disc jockeys showing off their LP and 45 rpm records, other people were simply about to take the next step or they lapsed into an unheard of condition, their solitude.

Family Party is not a dance photograph, though its jollity of movement would almost qualify it as such. Sidibé shot it close up to the partygoers and from slightly below them. They form a mass so tight within a space so narrow that the picture could have been titled *The Big Squeeze*. A few members of the chorus wanted to be taken as soloists, their heads poking out from behind bodies rubbed competitively together. Nowhere is there a figure old or authoritative—and therefore controlling—enough to be taken as a parent. Someone at the top of the crowd, his arms raised up, points downward with both hands, as if to signal who is who or what is what. At the moment, this gleeful man, who climaxes the party in the compositional sense, also gestures in outright communication with the photographer.

Still, one would care to know what kind of moment this was. Despite its general swing, it is not quite a moment of pleasure shared by everyone. The rhetoric of group portraiture is dominated by the metaphor of the shared, smiling moment. Here, the moment is disjointed by more private and reflective interludes, such as the curiosity of the two girls at the left, and the out of it, slightly sad demeanour of the young woman in the centre. We note three specifically variant psychologies, recorded by the opening of Sidibé's shutter: active engagement with the photographer, an intrigue with his process or mechanics, and consent to be his subject without thought of conforming to the scenario. For good measure, I should add another distraction—the impish little boy who has turned sidewise from the camera and grins knowingly at a man with sunglasses. Embosomed by the warmth and sweetness of the family, these anomalies make the picture.

In fact, the playfulness of the tableau is enhanced by such observed digressions from its theme. They provide touches of the unforeseen to what could easily have wound up as a monotonous and formulaic spectacle. Sidibé must have been aware of the fact that the complaisance of subjects stressed their play-acting over their reality. There was more to their lives than the charades that his camera stimulated and brought to the fore. As it happened, they posed with their obedient exuberance before a photographer who did not always want them to acknowledge his presence. How ironic that he valued self-enclosed and inner-directed behaviour, uncalled for by the occasion—and not collaborative by nature. Certainly, his practice was inherently a social business, and he relished his good standing in the community. Just the same, there were moments when the photographer and/or his subjects were psychologically on their own. It didn't matter so much whether the effect resulted from a mistiming of the shutter release, before or after people were ready for the taking of the image. These moments were worthy of being included because they contributed an intermittent piquancy of realism to the flowing artifice of the proceedings. The achievement of those moments came to the attention of Western critics and historians at a period—the 1980s—when departures from genre norms became a source of aesthetic interest. Photographs are, of course, mute, but in Sidibé's case, one feels one can almost hear them, as one moves through a panorama exhibiting his music of faces.

---

1   This remark is from a conversation between Sidibé and Andre Magnin in Bamako (1997): see Andre Magnin, *Malick Sidibé* (Zurich: Scalo, 1998).

Renzo Martens's
Episode III 'Enjoy Poverty'
(2008)

Collaboration is a term with a range of interpretations, some of them mutually antagonistic. While there are positive connotations attached to groups or individuals who work collaboratively, it requires only a shift in perspective to accuse or be accused of 'being a collaborator'. It is within this tension that we can consider Renzo Martens's difficult yet important film *Episode III: 'Enjoy Poverty'*. The films throws up a series of events centred around individual photographs, which are used by Martens to explore and, often, reproduce, tensions involved in collaboration.

Martens quickly and self-consciously establishes himself as the artist-protagonist, documentary film-maker and white Westerner touring the Democratic Republic of Congo (DRP) at the heart of the film. He arrives in the region by boat, a collection of porters carrying his substantial luggage of large metal boxes on their heads. He films himself in a straw hat and white shirt, reminiscent of the popular depictions of the colonial overseer or landowner. Early on, he meets a European plantation owner at a photographic exhibition of black-and-white images of Congolese plantation workers, images that mimic of the work of Sebastião Salgado. We discover that the plantation owner, whose employees populate the images, has just bought three of the photographs. This early encounter begins a process in which Martens demolishes any easy assumptions as to the efficacy of 'concerned photography' to ameliorate suffering. Through an interview with Martens, we learn that the same plantation owner considers it 'reasonable' that the children of his own employees are severely malnourished. >

Images on pp. 17–19: Stills from Episode III: 'Enjoy Poverty', dir. Renzo Martens, 2008

Moving on from the overtly aesthetic images of the exhibition, we encounter a group of white Western photojournalists as they are guided through an area of recent conflict where they have come to photograph the fighters and scattered corpses. Martens films the photographers, who seem to mimic each other—photographing the same fighters and the same corpses in the same eerily choreographed way. The photojournalists enter an abandoned village and discover a local photographic portrait studio, 'Studio Bolingo', with adverts for 'Paris style photographs'. Martens talks to a photographer who works for the news agency AFP, who explains that he earns 50 US dollars for every image sold. When Martens asks about the subjects of the photographs, and the part they played in the production of the image, the photographer remains adamant that he is the sole author, refusing any possibility that the people he photographed collaborated in the creation of the picture.

As the photojournalists move onto to the next 'newsworthy' story, Martens returns to Studio Bolingo to find the shop's owner. He meets a group of photographers, who tell him that each of the portraits they make is sold for 75 cents. Martens gathers the group together and explains that, working as local portrait photographers, they can expect to make one dollar profit per month. As photojournalists documenting the extreme poverty of the DRC, they could 'theoretically' make 1,000 dollars per month. What follows is among the most difficult parts of a film already saturated in terrible scenes. Martens takes the Congolese photographers and instructs them how to 'tap into' the resource of suffering and death that surrounds them. The photographs they take are brought to aid agency Médecins Sans Frontières (MSF), to seek permission to photograph in their hospitals. The MSF representative rejects the request, saying the photographs are no good and denouncing Martens and the Congolese for attempting to profit from them. The look of embarrassment and bemused anger on the faces of the local photographers is difficult to watch, particularly as it is clear that Martens knew his attempts to collaborate were destined to fail.

The deliberate construction of an unequal, even exploitative, relationship has been one of the main criticisms levelled at Martens's film. But to criticise the artist on the terms of his collaboration is to miss the point entirely. Martens's 'ironic' experiment to photographically exploit the region's poverty as a resource mirrors the structures of aid and exploitation that 'developed' nations force on countries such as the DRC. Through the film, we learn that aid money from Western institutions such as the World Bank is greater than the DRC's GDP and that, in some cases, 70–90% of that money flows back to the donor countries. The real and terrible irony here is that the systems that proclaim—not least through photojournalism—to help the people of DRC are directly responsible for perpetuating their suffering.

In the end, all forms of representation will fail. Or at least they fail if we continue to believe that there is some magic formula that will achieve a predictable relationship of cause and effect, imagery and action. The greatest myth of all concerns the capacity of images produced through documentary forms to 'do' anything at all. It is us, all of us, who are complicit in the continuing suffering in what has been termed the global south. We are all collaborators in its ongoing exploitation, and we have failed to collaborate with it. At the very least, Martens is honest about that.

"The real and terrible irony here is that the systems that proclaim—not least through photojournalism—to help the people of DRC are directly responsible for perpetuating their suffering."

Communities, Collectives, Collaborations: A Very Brief Introduction to Brighton Photo Biennial 2014

Mariama Attah

Lathigra/Sekgala 2014. A Photoworks, Market Photo Workshop, Joburg Photo
Umbrella and The Space co-commission for Brighton Photo Biennial 2014
supported by British Council Connect ZA programme

Brighton Photo Biennial 2014 explores issues of community, collectives and collaboration in photography, which it considers both as subjects and as modes of practice. Unlike previous editions of the Biennial, this one does not rely on the vision of an individual curator. Instead, Photoworks has worked in close partnership with a wide range of organisations and practitioners to develop a series of new projects and exhibitions. In part, the approach is rooted in necessity, as arts organisations operating in challenging times work strategically to pool resources.

At the same time, we recognised that such an approach contained many exciting possibilities. While the Biennial's overarching framework, and several of the key projects, reflect the research and interests of the Photoworks' team, from the formative stages the programme has been shaped by a multitude of voices and agendas. BPB14 results from a truly collaborative process, with all the problems and possibilities that the term suggests. It places particular importance on the commissioning and production of new work or on novel perspectives on re-presenting existing archival material.

An interest in the truth and fiction of photographic narratives sits at the core of the work, a theme that surfaces in the work of Jan von Holleben, whose play with perspectives places young collaborators at the heart of his artistic practice. The fantastical inventions take inspiration from the film collection at Hove Museum & Art Gallery to offer an imaginative route for children to try on different roles as subjects, assistants, creative researchers and critical consultants.

An interest in community sits at the core of the Reeves Project, which focuses on a photographic studio in the historic market town of Lewes. The history of the Reeves photography studio is reanimated, and its legacies made visible through site-specific installations on the high street it has occupied for four generations. A new collection of stories, recounted by members of the community, offers personal understandings of the role that the studio has played over the years.

Community involvement in further participatory projects enables learning across a wide range of groups. Widening Participation projects at the University of Brighton, the Mass Education project and Brighton & Hove Libraries projects provide a platform for self-guided learning and, in turn, for passing on acquired skills and knowledge. Programmes for young people include photography workshops led by trained undergraduates, artist-led workshops and drop-in sessions. The intergenerational exhibition programme focuses on collaborations between students from the University of Brighton and older people making a body of work promoting positive imagery and mutual understanding alongside the Families Programme, which offers a series of drop-in events and a one-day community photography festival. >

Communities

The theme of community informs several commissions in which the participation or involvement of particular groups is key. Kalpesh Lathigra and Thabiso Sekgala, for example, jointly map a photographic history of communities on the peripheries to explore issues around immigration. Sekgala documents the repercussions of forced removals from South African townships. Lathigra seeks out groups in both Laudium (an ex-Indian township) and areas of Brighton in order to highlight the role of the camera in these stories of immigrants.

Sirkka-Liisa Konttinen, *Girl on a 'Spacehopper'*,
1971, from the series *Byker*. Image courtesy
of Sirkka-Liisa Konttinen and Side Gallery

Collaboration

The collaborative element of the Biennial presents itself through a series of creative partnerships that expand and amplify key issues in photography. The multidisciplinary projects rely on collaboration as a tool for challenging artists and audiences alike.

Berlin-based artist Simon Faithfull explores the collapse and renewal of life-cycles, using the destructive nature of fire and the regenerative power of water. *REEF* revolves around the often unexpected outcomes of collaborative working, embracing the unknown and unknowable.

The Archive of Modern Conflict presents *Amore e Piombo: The Photography of Extremes in 1970s Italy*, an exhibition of slides, photographs and cuttings from its Rome press archives. This material has been selected to introduce visitors to the tumultuous 'Years of Lead': a period of widespread sociopolitical conflict and terrorism, characterised by collusions, coalition politics, intrigue and chaos.

Artist Erica Scourti works with video, performance and text to explore communication, connection and mediated intimacy in the networked age. She engages with the question of custodianship by working collaboratively with online communities to address the impact of new technologies on the photographic medium and its relationship to audiences. Pairing autobiographical content with the increasing self-awareness of online celebrities, Scourti questions ideas of authorship, ownership and online interactions.

Artist duo Cornford & Cross continue to explore a long-running interest in the relationship between photography and sculpture. Widening the realm of the collaborative team, artist Andrew Lacon has worked with and alongside the pair to consider the intersection between and representation of these art forms.

Ranging from the political to the practical, BPB14 presents exhibitions and projects that offer a variety of interpretations on community, collectives and collaborations. The opportunities that have arisen from these pairings are just the beginning of the collaborative process. The Biennial has stimulated debate and dialogue, provoking artists to create bodies of work that continue to define and defy our understanding of photography and its role in collaboration.

Collectives

Several of the Biennial exhibitions focus on the work of photography collectives, past and present, in order to explore the range of creative and political possibilities this mode of working involves. *5 Contemporary Photography Collectives* responds directly to the resurgence in photography collectives. The five collectives selected suggest a range of organisational structures and artistic ambitions. Elsewhere, the history of collectives is examined through material drawn from the Co-optic archives. Curated by Professor David Alan Mellor, the exhibition provides an insight into a neglected corner of the culture of photography in Britain.

A new commission sees anthropologist Elizabeth Edwards and artists Hannah Starkey and Uriel Orlow explore the archives of the famous Magnum agency, which was established as a co-operative in 1947. They will re-present Magnum's photographic history, based on their areas of expertise, knowledge and skills. A further ten new commissions explore the topic of sustainable living, with a series of photo essays presented as site-specific installations throughout Brighton and Hove.

Connect/ Disconnect

KALPESH LATHIGRA & THABISO SEKGALA

in

conversation

with

CELIA DAVIES & JOHN FLEETWOOD

All images: Lathigra/Sekgala 2014. A Photoworks, Market Photo Workshop,
Joburg Photo Umbrella and The Space co-commission for Brighton Photo
Biennial 2014 supported by British Council Connect ZA programme

CD: CD: We have chosen the concept of collaboration as a starting point to generate a new photography project. The brief is very simple: two photographers working together, across two locations—the UK and South Africa—to make a joint project. So, let's talk about the process.

KL: I really welcome the idea of collaboration. I've never worked in a collaborative process, so, from a personal point of view, it is exciting, and gives me food for thought. It also lets me feel on a very personal level that I am evolving my practice, with an aspect of learning from another photographer, and being challenged by that and my own perceptions about my own practice.

JF: There's something about the setting up of a collaboration between two photographers that's somehow like a blind date. I'm interested in how you started to talk about the project—how does the process of collaboration enter into how you determine outputs of the work collectively? So, we're talking about process—how you make this work together. But we're also talking about exhibition—how you select work, edit. What considerations did this pose?

TS: For me, the idea of collaboration presented the opportunity to be brave, and to be contented about the idea of collaboration itself. I was interested in this idea of contribution and sharing.

KL: Neither Thabiso nor I knew each other, and not being loaded with other people's work in your mind brings about its own specialness—the fact that such a collaboration is very open, and also the process of a combined project where you are in many ways forced to really challenge yourself. It's quite liberating to say, 'OK you know what, hand it over', so you can look at each other's stuff, and have a free-flowing dialogue about each other's work and ideas. My practice has moved from editorial to commercial to fine art, and this mixes it all up. I guess I would say my practice is more immediate, but when I look at Thabiso's practice there's this meditative kind of peace to his work.

TS: For me, the thing that came to mind when I started to have a conversation with Kalpesh was this idea of identity: the identity that I have as a photographer and the identity that he has as a photographer. I mean both our literal identity as people and also our identity in terms of our signature styles of working and approach. Something I thought about a lot when I was asked to make a collaborative work was the idea of authorship. How, if I work with somebody else, do we have a voice that is one but at the same time reflects our different ways of looking at things?

JF: Can you talk a bit more about authorship—where is it located and how do you deal with it?

TS: I think the issue of authorship is very difficult because Kalpesh's work is similar to mine. It's still a challenge how we're going to make a distinct kind of divide: this is mine, this is yours, and it should appear differently. A question that Celia asked us is still unanswered: are we going to separate the work or going to mix it? I've seen a lot of collaborations labelled with photographers' names where the book or exhibition was just one thing and it didn't matter who did what. Like that between Broomberg and Chanarin, who have been working together for a long time: when you look at their work it's always a unity, you don't see two photographers; it's more like a composite.

KL: When you're working in a collaboration or as a collective, all that matters is the work. We were talking about editing—how we should edit—and I think that's a negotiation; you're negotiating that kind of partnership together.

CD: OK, so you've both identified that this is a new way of working for you, opening up new dialogues. What are the potential challenges or compromises for you as you make the work?

KL: You have the challenge of logistics and sharing time. I think for me that's the biggest challenge because I've always worked as a single entity, and I always plan and research everything beforehand, so I know what I'm going to do when I'm ready to hit the ground. Now, I'm having to take on board Thabiso—what he needs to do, what his plans are—and we need to combine our approaches so that we have a working relationship.

TB: For me, it's a process of formulating a strategy too. I have my own ideas, but they also evolve around Kalpesh's ideas. So, when Kalpesh said he was interested in Indian communities, it wasn't my initial thought—but I became curious about Indian communities in South Africa, and then wanted to create my own stories. It's something I've never thought to do as a project.

KL: When you have someone like Thabiso whose process is organic, it allows you to stop, think, process and try to understand how that collaboration will take place. The questions I initially asked were: Should we sit down and edit together? Should we have a narrative? But on consideration, maybe not—let's not be so linear. Let's think about this in a more elegant way.

CD: How are you dealing with the two different locations and the two very different contexts to make two exhibitions? How is this circling in your mind's eye in terms of how to take photographs, what to take photographs of and what the potential output of that would be?

KL: I think until you're in a physical location you just never know how you're going to react to it. In Laudium I noticed roads like Kashmir Avenue and Emerald Avenue. Celia had spoken about the Brighton Pavilion, so I visited it, and thought, 'This is interesting, the idea of exporting cultures.' There's something very relevant here about immigrants, communities and these little links to colonialism that come in. And that changed my perspective. I think that's going to be the challenge at the end of this project, making this thread apparent through the work.

CD: And Thabiso—and I'm conscious that you haven't been to Brighton yet—what's your thinking at the moment?

TS: When I started to consider the idea of Pretoria West, I found myself thinking about the usual kinds of stories, 'Oh, you can see the place has changed and people have moved from this place to that.' But I also realised that this was not the most important story because it's one we all know. When I started thinking about it, I needed some sort of current affairs idea of looking at these places. I thought about *lost love* because it would give me the freedom to not just focus on one particular story. 'Lost love' adverts are something you see on many streets in Johannesburg or Pretoria, offering their services to people who have lost their lovers. So I think for me lost love ties in perfectly with the idea of me looking at the history of the place we are photographing, in Marabastad and Laudium. I think there is sense of lost love through people forcefully removed from places, due to the Group Areas Act.

Although from the beginning I didn't want to be led by research, what fascinated me was the image of soldiers in Brighton Pavilion, which used as an Indian military hospital in WW1. And I thought about this when I was in Marabastad in South Africa; so, the relationship of being in a place where you don't belong to that of being in a place where you think you belong. I kept thinking about these ideas about disconnection and belonging.

JF: Do you see this collaboration as an opportunity for similar ideas to be explored or is it an opportunity to explore together contradiction and complementary ideas you have in photographing the same places and subjects?

TS: I think for me it's both.

KL: Yeah, there's been respectful debate of each other's positions, and I think that's the thing: compromise and giving and taking. And it's also listening. So even when we're not agreeing, both of us go away and think and then come back, and suddenly our ideas might complement each other. I think, sometimes, people can be too aggressive with their 'I'm going to do this because this is what I believe' attitudes, unwilling to sit back and actually listen to somebody else's ideas. On a personal level, I think that affects my work because I want to listen, I want to learn, and I'm willing to give way.

TS: I think for me also this collaboration is a cure for my prejudice. As a photographer, you've been talking, telling and giving advice, and you—as in your practice—from having worked in, say, photojournalism, may have shifted to editorial and perhaps, more recently, fine arts. And my prejudice could be: 'Oh, I'm this kind of photographer, I'm not that kind of photographer.' And sometimes when you work with people you start to learn that all these definitions can really hold you back. My expectation or hope is that if I take part in this collaborative process, maybe my work will be a different type of work.

CD: Through various discussions we have had on Skype to develop the content for this project you identified communities in both Johannesburg and Brighton that you would like to work with. Could you expand on this.

KL: I think the conversations we've had via Skype had a profound and positive impact. But what drew me to the idea of the Indian community in South Africa was anger. In the images I've seen coming out of South Africa I notice that Indians are invisible or at least underrepresented in photography and the visual arts more generally. When I looked at Broomberg and Chanarin's work and at Pieter Hugo's stuff, I thought to myself: 'Wait a minute. How can a community that's been in South Africa longer than the Indian community has been in Britain not have any kind of visual representation in contemporary South Africa?' So I looked at archives and I found a thing in *Drum* magazine—I saw these images, and thought: 'These Indians have been there for that long!' The processes of immigration have evolved and have changed, and, culturally, Indians are kind of embedded in South Africa. But why is that not shown?

        My hope is that the work will show these communities as being part of South Africa, whatever the tensions or non-tensions that exist for them; it will make them visible. I don't want this to sound like a cliché, but I just want some kind of recognition: that these communities are here, that they are a part of the wider South Africa.

TS: Marabastad is such a small place—you can overlook it or pass through it without noticing. My interest in Marabastad is a personal one, and it has changed a lot in the past seven years. When we went to Laudium, we met an old guy who said he used to live there, and he told us what it used to be like. I'm always interested in changes to places. But mainly I'm interested in the idea of amnesia—what we choose to remember and what we choose to forget. I think this is especially true in South Africa where commemoration is commonplace.

KL: See, Thabiso says 'amnesia'. It's so poetic! With this collaboration, in how it works, he brings to it this kind of essence, whereas I'm thinking 'I can't emotionally express this', as I'm quite literal. And that word 'amnesia' expresses what's changing, and meshes with what I'm trying to do with my work, photographically. I may not literally speak about it, but the emotive relevance has exactly the same overtones.

JF: I'm interested in the issues surrounding the silence of minorities within South Africa and how it is that these voices were muted. But are you thinking about that in terms of Brighton because in South Africa these things are quite explicit perhaps?

KL: Early on in my career I remember photographing World War II Sikh soldiers as a project. Some Indian and West Indian veterans fought for their mother country, Britain. And yet this has largely been forgotten. I think there is a kind of silence there. Brighton has a rich history, and I'm intending that the narrative about immigrants will also include the importance of the historical nature of the soldiers, and adding on top of that additional factors: Why was the Prince Regent so interested in Orientalism? Why did he have all this stuff in the Brighton Pavilion? It will be interesting to understand the underlying processes.

CD: I think this has also been answered to some extent: in working together, is there an opportunity to develop a critique around the work with your collaborator?

KL: I think the critique is in the fact that you have somebody else sitting alongside you, looking at your work and talking to you, and bringing their voice, opinions, thought processes and understanding. They will read your work differently from you. It's always been said that you can be too close to your work—you need somebody to stand back and look at it and understand you from their perspective. And I think with Thabiso I couldn't have asked for a better collaborative partner, because he's the absolute opposite of what I am.

JF: To what extent do you see the people you photograph as collaborators in your work?

KL: I think they are your collaborative partners because you are affected by them in many ways by speaking to them, learning more about their histories, their language.

TS: I have also been considering these ideas. I don't know how to approach this exactly, but I was thinking about bringing people and the voices of people together by asking questions or having interviews or conversations.

CD: So, in terms of people collaborating in this, you both seem quite open to a dialogue being represented intrinsically in the final work?

TS: Yeah, I also see this as an opportunity to not only look at photography but also examine photography in relation to text among many other things.

KL: I think captioning is going to play a vital part. If you put captions underneath the pictures and they contradict the imagery, I wonder how that will play upon the viewer. It's quite exciting to kind of think about those things!

CD: There seems to be a willingness around adapting the various outputs, whether photographs, film or text, so you're actually representing the stories and subjects from your findings?

KL: Yes. I think we always agreed that this commission was a great foundation for something bigger for us. That's also reflected in the nature of mediums, whether it's photography, film or writing. There's much more collaboration going on today than there was five or ten years ago. And I think people are much more willing to adapt and work on projects together and are excited about the outcomes. It's about having an openness to let something grow and to let it move you forwards.

Real Britain 1974:
The Co-optic Project

David Alan Mellor
& Geraldine Alexander

Co-optic was a London-based collective of photographers established in 1973. At its peak, it boasted 120 members, many of whom went on to build high-profile careers in photography and art. David Alan Mellor and Geraldine Alexander take a look at this largely neglected corner of the history of 'Independent Photography' in Britain.

Paul Hill, *Enoch Powell Electioneering*, 1970.
First edition of *Real Britain Postcards*, printed 1974. © Co-optic

By 1974 documentary realism had a special prominence in English television, film and photography. This exhibition celebrates the 40th anniversary of the launching of the Co-optic group's *Real Britain Postcard* project. It laid claim to combine the new 'independent photography', which was inspired by US examples, with the style and forms of 1960s photo-journalism, to establish a more authentic representation of contemporary life in Britain.

The group comprised some of the emerging practitioners of the time, including Martin Parr, Daniel Meadows, Sirkka-Liisa Konttinen, Nick Hedges, Fay Godwin, Paul Hill, Ron McCormick and Gerry Badger. It was driven by the organisational skills of fellow photographer and entrepreneur Stephen Weiss.

The BPB14 exhibition uncovers a lost episode in the development of social-documentary British photography. It draws on the Co-optic archive, featuring original prints donated by the photographers, as well as prints from the *Real Britain Postcard* project.

This will be the first public showing of this material from the Co-optic archive; it includes photographs, posters, newsletters and ephemera related to seminars, exhibitions and events organised by Co-optic, alongside the *Real Britain Postcard* project: a two-part edition of 25 photographic postcards.

David Mellor

Co-optic

Co-optic was a London-based collective of photographers conceived in 1972 and launched officially in June 1973.[1] It was the creation of businessman and self-taught photographer Stephen Weiss, following discussions with enthusiasts including Gerry Badger, Peter Baistow, Neil Gulliver, Peter Turner, Martin Stanley and James Fahey (who, together, formed Co-optic's first executive). As a co-operative, the group aimed to progress along voluntary and democratic lines: owned and run by its members, any profits from activities—including seminars, exhibitions, and publications—were used to fund future projects.

The early success of Co-optic was due, in part, to Weiss's business acumen, motivational skills and financial resources. Its success was also a product of the wave of optimism about photography's evolving status as a creative occupation in Britain during the 1970s—a feeling shared by many of its members. Other initiatives helped to foster this emerging culture of independent photography, including Spectro Arts in Whitley Bay, the Side Gallery in Newcastle, West Midlands Arts and the Half Moon Gallery in London's East End.

The group aimed to produce a forum in which its extensive network of photographers would be able to gather and discuss ideas and activities. Although most members were based in the capital, some hailed from the provinces, while others came from as far afield as Germany, Sri Lanka, Sweden and America. Weiss was highly ambitious, and set out to enlist some significant established and emerging names. They included Bill Brandt, Dorothy Bohm, David Hurn, Paddy Summerfield and Ken Baird. Other prominent names from the arts and education included Nick Serota, Barry Lane, Paul Hill and Bill Gaskin. Many became members, while others offered external support.

At its peak, Co-optic boasted a membership of 120. It predominantly attracted young male professionals, many of them photojournalists, most with a technical or art school background. Women or mature professionals were less well represented. Fay Godwin was a notable exception who, at the outset of her career and still pursuing wider opportunities through her literary portrait practice, was drawn to the group out of a sense of 'isolation'.

Monthly newsletters provided the main form of communication. These featured administrative matters, group project updates and reviews, a diary of upcoming events, practical advice such as 'exhibiting strategies' or 'sales techniques', and updated contact details for all members. A slide archive was established and registered on the National Photographic Record, which, by 1975, numbered 700 slides. The option of a reduced membership fee of £5 and three prints, rather than the usual £7.50, helped a small print collection to develop. Further funds were raised through a print auction, held at the Photographers' Gallery in December 1976.[2] >

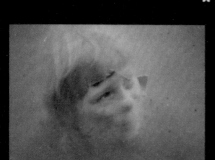

Nick Hedges, *For Shelter*, Salford, Lancashire.
First edition of the *Real Britain Postcards*, printed 1974. © Co-optic

Stephen Weiss, *Cricket Power, Acton.*
First edition of the *Real Britain Postcards*, printed 1974. © Co-optic

Seminars and Exhibitions

The emphasis on self-organisation led some members to form their own interest groups, which organised a range of events and activities. Some managed to draw people out of London: Richard Wood's two-day seminar on 'Equivalence in photography', for example, attracted 22 members along with partners and friends to West Runton, Norfolk. Peter Turner ran a series of seminars from his home in south London with the explicit aim of sharpening critical responses to contemporary photography. As the editor of *Creative Camera*, Turner brought other benefits to the group: discounts on all *Creative Camera* publications and opportunities for members to participate in upcoming events, including Jean-Claude Lemagny's selection of contemporary British photography for Paris's *Bibliotheque Nationale* in 1974. As the art director at *New Society*, Peter Baistow provided Co-optic photographers with opportunities to contribute their work to the journal.[3]

Co-optic exhibitions varied both in their size and how they were organised. Participants in *Ten from Co-optic* (February–November 1974), for example, were selected by a group vote. The exhibition travelled the UK and finished in Essen, Germany. *Friends* (11 November–18 December 1974), staged at the Half Moon Gallery, was open to all. *Camden Photographers* at the Shaw Theatre in London's Euston Road (July 1975) and *Leisure in Camden* at Swiss Cottage Library (October 1975) were more local events organised by Fay Godwin and Gerry Badger.

Co-optic also played a supporting role in Mark Edwards and Chris Steele Perkins's exhibition *Young British Photographers*. This opened at the Museum of Modern Art, Oxford in January 1975, touring the UK before showing at its final venue, the Visual Studies Workshop in Rochester, New York. Twelve of its 14 participants were Co-optic members. With the aid of an Arts Council grant, Co-optic also published and distributed the show's catalogue.

Real Britain

Co-optic's opening offer to prospective members included an invitation to participate in its most successful scheme: the *Real Britain Postcards* project. This involved a two-part edition of 25 photographic postcards, published in December 1974.

Postcards proved to be popular items in the resurgence of ephemera that took place during the 1970s. The Arts Council had used them in its *Two Views* exhibition in 1972. They also featured in student assignments and regional Arts group competitions. The London gallerist Anthony Stokes recalls using invitations that doubled as postcards as part of his wider promotional and sales strategy.[4]

The *Real Britain Postcards* offered an effective public platform for creative expression, but were also relatively cheap to produce. This meant they provided a steady source of income for the group. The first editions of some 50,000 cards sold out within a year, followed by a reprint. They were also selected by the Design Council for its exhibition *Shopping in Britain* in 1975.

The images were selected by a group vote. As monochrome remained the preferred aesthetic of the period, the *Real Britain Postcards* showed a nation in black and white. A significant percentage of the images portray the same nostalgic or humorous projections of Britain seen in the photographs of Tony Ray-Jones from the previous decade. Other photographs mirrored the dominant schools and styles taught on photographic courses at the time, including the language of American 'street photography', traces of European surrealism, the English tradition of *Picture Post*, and Humphrey Spender's work in the Mass-Observation project. >

Martin Parr, *Blackpool*, 1971.
First edition of *Real Britain Postcards*, printed 1974. © Co-optic

Homer Sykes, *John Knill, Ceremony*, 1971.
First edition of *Real Britain Postcards*, printed 1974. © Co-optic

Demise

The dearth of sponsorship or institutional support for photography in Britain during the early 1970s led an emerging network of groups and individuals to look to each for support. The Co-optic membership overlapped with that of the Half Moon Gallery, and, from the end of 1974, ideas about the sharing of events, facilities and contacts featured with increasing regularity in the Co-optic newsletters. Indeed, in 1975, the organisations did collaborate on 'Camera obscured? Perspectives on contemporary British photography', a series of six seminars aimed at provoking a wider debate about the creation of better opportunities for photographers across the sociocultural spectrum.

Government grants and sponsorship were a vital mainstay for many small groups and galleries during the period, and, as finances were tightly restricted, there was stiff competition for eligibility. The sober tone of Co-optic's annual report of 1975 brought a difficult year to a close. It suggests a group caught at a crossroads as it tried to redefine its role from part-time amateur organisation to full-time and professional. It had looked to the Arts Council for support, and channelled its energies into publishing and distribution. Once again, it speculated on the pragmatic benefits of sharing a permanent base with the Half Moon Gallery: 'Half Moon providing a local and community focus… Co-optic providing the broad, national focus'. These plans were never realised. The Half Moon Gallery joined forces with Terry Dennett and Jo Spence's Photography Workshop in 1975, to become the influential Half Moon Photography Workshop.

At the beginning of 1976, the first issue of *Bellows III* was published as a prototype for a new Co-optic journal. This laid out the new profile required of the group if it was to meet the criteria for Arts Council support. Despite efforts including the appointment of a full-time co-ordinator, the group began to disintegrate. The final blow came from the failure of a fourth application for Arts Council support. Co-optic ceased operations in April 1977. An exchange of letters published in the *British Journal of Photography* revealed Weiss's frustration and anger that an organisation which had vast potential for the good of British photography had been allowed to die.

A few managed to catch a more authentic spirit of the 1970s. Sirkka-Liisa Konttinen's *Girl on a 'Spacehopper'* (1971), for example, used a glamorised young subject to personify the destruction of the wrecking ball that ripped through the heart of the old Byker community. Bruce Rae's *Earls Court Queen* (1973) captured the changing cultural values of the 1970s with its references to shifting sexual politics and the emerging subculture in the music, art and fashion scenes of London and New York.

The main criticism of the images came from within Co-optic. Daniel Meadows's comments on the narrowness and repetition of the subject matter echoing David Kilpatrick's earlier complaint about the narrow and dated selection of photographers, in *Ten From Co-optic*. In that instance, Weiss had recognised the charge of 'conservatism', and agreed that, in future, a more 'pioneering direction ought to be struck'.

Other criticisms came from the press. Writing in *The Guardian*, Euan Duff attacked the work produced by the Young British Photographers, six of whom featured in the *Real Britain Postcards*: he accused them of working 'in a vacuum', and stated they were 'self-deluding in regarding themselves as the vanguard of a new movement, when they are in fact, the rearguard of a tired old movement that reached its peak before many of them were born'. Duff was also critical of the Arts Council for supporting the work.

1   All information unless otherwise stated is from the author's research of the Co-optic Archive (2010–11), with the kind permission of its owner, Stephen Weiss.

2   A brief record of this event can be found on Homer Syke's website.
3   Barry Lane, interview with the author (11 March 2010).

4   Anthony Stokes, correspondence with the author (31 January 2011).

REAL BRITAIN
POSTCARDS

'Glyndebourne, 1967' photograph by Tony Ray-Jones
Number 4, first edition Real Britain Postcards
© **Co-optic, 1974. Printed in England**

Five Contem-porary Photography Collectives

ABC

BURN
MY EYE

RUIDO
PHOTO

SPUTNIK
PHOTOS

UNCERTAIN
STATES

By banding together we provide each other with some
of the support that a traditional publisher might provide, but
without the need to compromise our individual visions.

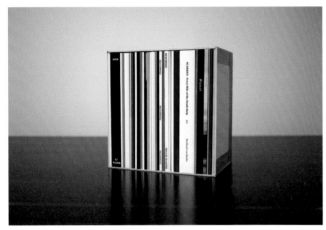

Collection of ABC publications

San Andres, TX, from the book *Pumped*
by Mishka Henner, 2012

Who are you?

Louis Porter: I am a photographer and an artist who makes and collects books.

Andreas Schmidt: My name is Andreas Schmidt. The last time I checked the German online phone book, there were more than 4,000 search results for that name. More than 100 Andreas Schmidts live in Berlin alone. My first self-published artist book *38 Andreas Schmidt* dealt with this subject.

Travis Shaffer: I'm an artist, a book maker, an educator, and a photographer … of sorts.

We are all part of Artists' Books Cooperative (ABC). ABC currently comprises 18 artists: Andreas Schmidt, David Schulz, Duncan Wooldridge, EJ Major, Eric Doeringer, Erik Benjamins, Fred Free, Heidi Neilson, Hermann Zschiegner, Jonathan Lewis, Joshua Deaner, Louis Porter, Mishka Henner, Oliver Griffin, Paul Soulellis, Tanja Lažetic, Travis Shaffer and Wil van Iersel.

Where are you from?

TS: I am ABC's resident landlocked American—currently based in Columbia, Missouri, where I am on the art faculty at the University of Missouri.

LP: I'm originally from the UK but I've been living in Australia since 2000 and have recently returned to live in London.

AS: I was born in the most heavily bombed German city (per capita) during the Second World War, but have lived in London for the last 20 years (also heavily bombed during the Second World War). I have never been involved in a war.

LP: The remaining members of ABC live in London, Amsterdam, Manchester, Culver City, New York, New Port Beach, Walla Walla, Brookline, Long Island, Millburn, Providence and Ljubljana.

How long have you been doing this?

AS: ABC was founded in December 2009.

I was one of the founding members. Sort of second or third in command after the Godfather, to use a Mafia analogy.

LP: I joined on 14 February 2014—exactly 102 years after Arizona became the 48th State of the USA, I became the 16th member of ABC.

TS: I joined in January 2010. In late 2009, a founding member posted a comment on my POD book *NYSE:CBL Mall Maps*. The comment simply provided a link to ABC's website. I promptly inquired about membership, and received this in response: 'The procedure of becoming a member is quite simple. I'll ask all members of the network to have a look at your books. They'll say yes or no. If the majority says yes, you are in.'

Four years have passed since. Much has changed; however, the application procedure is essentially the same.

Apes as Lovers, from the book *Aped* by E. J. Major, 2012

ABCED poster for the Gagosian Gallery, New York, March–April 2013

What do you do?

TS: Our interactions centre around various book fairs, exhibitions and an online forum. We each operate independently as artists, but we have been known to collaborate.

AS: *ABCED*—the first multi-volume book project created by members of ABC—celebrated Ed Ruscha's 75th birthday. This work was an open-edition boxed set of 33 books available only during Ed Ruscha's 75th year. Since Ed is now 76, the set is no longer available.

LP: We are currently working on our second collaborative project, *ABCEUM*, which will be released in late 2014. We can't say too much about it at this stage, but rest assured there'll be a cafe.

TS: The nexus of ABC is the online forum—an encyclopaedic repository of all group discussion dating back to our founding days, it includes our ideas, [dis]agreements, rants, and all secretive and arcane processes required to make an artist book.

Why do you work as a collective?

LP: Self-publishing can seem like working in the vacuum of space, fighting against insurmountable odds. By banding together we provide each other with some of the support that a traditional publisher might provide, but without the need to compromise our individual visions. There are several practical benefits to this arrangement: we have 'repositories' in member's homes on either side of the Atlantic, the cost of stalls at book fairs is split across the group, and a collaborative project can be ambitious in its scope, without taking 20 years to complete.

Like any democratic organisation, ABC has its fair share of minor disagreements that occasionally impede the smooth running of its cultural operations. Militant splinter groups and blood feuds aside, the general tone is always underscored by the strong respect we have for each other's work.

AS: The best bit of being a part of ABC is that you surround yourself with like-minded lunatics. It's like Alcoholics Anonymous for book makers!

BURN MY EYE

Jason Penner

As we see it, a collective can consistently create interesting work if and only if it cultivates its greatest differences while cherishing a common vision; in other words, when a collective seeks for itself an unstable equilibrium.

Juichi Nishimura

Zisis Kardianos

Justin Vogel

J. B. Maher

Who are you?

Burn My Eye is a collective of 14 photographers who define themselves as lovers of unposed photography. We share a determination to photograph our surroundings and express ourselves through the act of photographing. Even though we share the same literacy regarding photography, each of us has a particular sensibility. The collective is enriched by many singular bodies of work, from surreal street photography to elastic candid photography, in passing-by public spaces and images of people.

Where are you from?

Burn My Eye counts people from seven different nationalities spread over eight different countries among its members: the USA, the UK, Greece, Ireland, France, Taiwan, Japan and Canada. Some of us studied photography and cinema formally, but most of us came to photography in recent years.

How long have you been doing this?

We met some years ago on the Flickr group Hardcore Street Photography. In 2011, we decided to create a private group to discuss and launch projects. Burn My Eye went public in December 2011.

What do you do?

We don't have a particular operating mode, except perhaps for self-management. When a member proposes a project, the other members usually engage with it, and the proposing member acts as a manager of sorts. This year, we have been invited to participate in three photography festivals, almost at the same time. Though we have already collectively worked on several projects and exhibitions, this is a huge change in scale for the collective. We are in a state of transition.

Burn My Eye is currently working on two series. *The Road Home* (working title) consists of images collected within a short distance from our relative homes over a lengthy period. *The 24hr Project* uses images made by each photographer on one particular day, with the proviso that individuals can make as many attempts they feel are required at forming a cohesive set. These are obviously differentiated by time scale, and are intended to stretch our capabilities in both the way they are shot and in the editing process. We are looking forward to publishing two rich sets of pictures that will push and pull the audience across cultural, socio-economic and stylistic boundaries.

Why do you work as a collective?

A collective is enriched by different sensibilities, allowing engagement with a wide variety of photographic series and opinions. Usually when exploring a particular field, a photographer has a single type of work. As we see it, a collective can consistently create interesting work if and only if it cultivates its greatest differences while cherishing a common vision; in other words, when a collective seeks for itself an unstable equilibrium. A collective is like a musical band. We are friends, first and foremost. The most difficult thing is to mature towards a more rigorous way of working.

RUIDO PHOTO

From *La Sala Negra* by Pau Coll and Edu Ponces

We established the collective as an alternative,
to create a brand and join forces to support
and produce the type of photography we believe in.

From the project *En El Camino* by Toni Arnau, Edu Ponces and Edu Soteras

Who are you?

RUIDO Photo is a group dedicated to documentary photography, journalism and documentary with a human rights perspective. We comprise three photographers, Toni Arnau, Pau Coll and Edu Ponces; a journalist, Alejandra Cukar; a designer, Roger Pérez Gironés; and some contributors doing tasks of fundraising, web programming, video postproduction or social work.

Our organisation was founded in 2004 and is committed to in-depth documentary projects that show stories that regularly appear in the mass media. RUIDO Photo also produces outreach materials such as books, documentaries and exhibitions that aim to influence society and provoke reflection and positive social change.

Where are you from?

The core members of RUIDO Photo are from Spain and Argentina, but we have contributors from different countries, such as Brazil, Italy, El Salvador and Mexico, among others.

How long have you been doing this?

RUIDO Photo was founded in 2004 from a group of students interested in social documentary photography. The current members of the organisation all joined within a year of its foundation.

From *A Silent Death* by Toni Arnau

From *La Sala Negra* by Pau Coll and Edu Ponces

From *La Sala Negra* by Pau Coll and Edu Ponces

What do you do?

RUIDO Photo focuses on the ability of photography to generate reflection and social transformation. Our journalistic and documentary projects deal with serious social problems and human rights violations, addressing them in depth and through long-term research.

Since 2004, RUIDO Photo has been transformed into an organisation with documentary projects realised in more than 20 countries. This has resulted in four photography books, four audio-visual documentaries and dozens of exhibitions and social projects that aim to raise awareness or to use photography as a tool for social transformation. Our photos have been published around the world in publications including *Time Magazine* (USA), *El Pais* (Spain), *Folha de São Paulo* (Brazil), *Miami Herald* (USA), *Proceso* (Mexico) and *El Faro* (El Salvador). Our work has also received a range of international awards. RUIDO Photo also publishes the main digital magazine of photography in Spain: *7.7* (www.7dot7.com).

One of our most prominent projects, *Orilleros*, combines photography and journalistic reporting on the crisis affecting the population living along the South American river Paraná that has resulted from environmental degradation brought about by private interests. Another project, *Sala Negra*, focused on social violence in Central America. *En el Camino* looked at the journey of undocumented migrants crossing Mexico *en route* to the EEUU.

Why do you work as a collective?

We, as members of RUIDO Photo, have worked as a collective since the beginning of our professional careers. We are all between 30 and 35 years old, and part of the generation which found that traditional media no longer supported or took risks on quality documentary photography and in-depth photojournalism. We established the collective as an alternative, to create a brand and to join forces to support and produce the type of photography we believe in. This union has given us the space to produce works with much greater depth than we could alone. It has also become a reference of quality for media and agencies. The horizontal structure of the collective allows us to participate in all professional decisions—and have fun while doing our work.

SPUTNIK PHOTOS

Jan Brykczynski

In a collective everything is easier—
exchanging ideas, looking for money, working on
projects and exhibitions, creating books.

From *The Winners* by Rafal Milach

What do you do?
We are registered as an NGO in Poland. We observe and describe what surrounds us, especially our common experience of living in Central and Eastern Europe in the post-transformation period. Together we have organised several dozen exhibitions around the world; our projects have been featured at photography festivals and in international magazines. We have published several books. Now we are running a long-term mentoring programme for young photographers.

Why do you work as a collective?
In a collective everything is easier—exchanging ideas, looking for money, working on projects and exhibitions, creating books. We are supported by great journalists, curators, a graphic designer, a project co-ordinator, and a PR manager, when necessary. So, we have more time to work on photos and develop our creative ideas. When we need to find a frame for a project, that gives all of us the maximum possible freedom.

Who are you?
I am Agnieszka Rayss, one of the founders of Sputnik Photos. Sputnik is made up of eight other photographers: Andrej Balco, Jan Brykczynski, Manca Juvan, Andrei Liankevich, Michal Luczak, Justyna Mielnikiewicz, Rafal Milach and Adam Panczuk.

Where are you from?
We are documentary photographers from Central and Eastern Europe—Poland, Slovakia, Slovenia, Belarus, Georgia.

How long have you been doing this?
Our international collective was founded in 2006.

From *I Reminisce and Cry for Life* by Agnieszka Rayss

From *I Reminisce and Cry for Life* by Agnieszka Rayss

From *I Am In Vogue* by Adam Panczuk

UNCERTAIN STATES

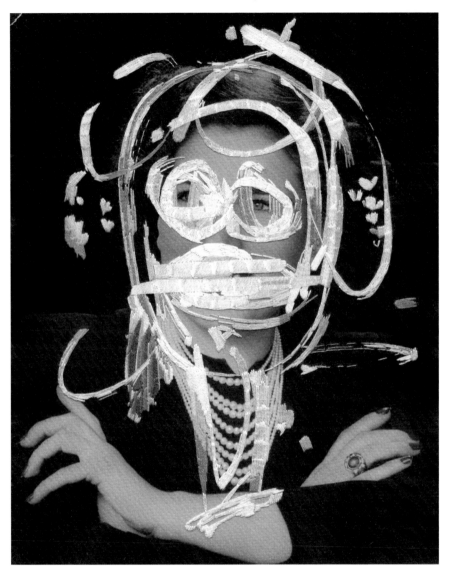

Contemplation by Julie Cockburn, 2014

When you collaborate, you are taken out of a place
of safety and encouraged to see things in a new way.
Collaboration relies on openness and knowledge-
sharing but, most importantly, it requires trust: trust
between us and trust in the creative process that
is clearly always in a slightly uncertain state.

Untitled by Karl Ohiri, 2013

Barnabé by Agatha A. Nitecka, 2013

Who are you?

We are David George, Spencer Rowell and Fiona Yaron-Field. We are the co-founders of the Uncertain States project. We have over 100 other artists and writers affiliated to us who at some time have been involved with the project over the past four and a half years.

Where are you from?

We are based in London.

How long have you been doing this?

Uncertain States started in 2009, publishing a broadsheet and exhibiting work. Since December 2010 we have held 'Salon Talks' on the first Tuesday of each month. Our first collaboration with an external organisation took place in 2012, when we worked with Photovoice. In September 2013 we held our first public panel discussion, at The Victoria and Albert Museum, London. In 2013 we received Arts Council funding that enabled us to distribute the broadsheet to key museums and galleries across the UK. In 2014 we launched print sales in collaboration with Four Corners and the Metro Imaging lab.

Daisy, Wamphray by Robin Grierson, 2006

What do you do?

Uncertain States is an artist-led project that publishes and distributes a free quarterly broadsheet newspaper promoting discussion in and around contemporary British lens-based art. We hold monthly talks that focus on contemporary photography. We organise and curate an annual exhibition to showcase our contributors' work. We also manage a website where all the papers can be viewed on line.

We—David, Spencer and Fiona—steer the running of all the activities of Uncertain States, but we are heavily supported by the other artists who help in the success of the project. The network of people involved uses its resources and contacts to push events forward.

As the editorial team, we organise, select photographers and curate the paper. We take responsibility for production, we employ the designer, liaise and oversee the printing of the paper. For the last six months we have been joined by Mary George, a curator, to help organise and oversee various projects. We are now establishing print sales. After an initial exhibition to launch the work, all the prints will be on sale via an online gallery. The prints will be of limited edition, and embossed. We are organising an open call with nine prestigious selectors: the finalists will be published in the paper, and there will be an exhibition of the work. It is also a great opportunity for the entrants to have their work seen and chosen by the selectors.

Why do you work as a collective?

Our original purpose in setting up the paper was to create a platform that would support and develop each artist's individual practice. Only later did it become clear that the project could also support and develop other lens-based artists too. Working collaboratively enables you to draw upon a knowledge base that would otherwise be inaccessible, as each of us brings our own unique set of skills. Through this collaboration, new relationships have been formed and new audiences developed.

Working alone had been isolating, and it was particularly difficult to maintain stamina and a good sense of one's own artistic practice. But it is not always easy working together, as it challenges your own sense of how things should be done and forces you to accept other people's viewpoints and perspectives. This balance between opening yourself to something new and different and not losing your own position is a demanding and interesting challenge.

When you collaborate, you are taken out of a place of safety and encouraged to see things in a new way. Collaboration relies on openness and knowledge-sharing but, most importantly, it requires trust: trust between us and trust in the creative process that is clearly always in a slightly uncertain state.

Red Shoes by Lydia Goldblatt, 2012

Sinking, Feeling

SIMON FAITHFULL
REEF

Text by
BRIAN DILLON

Simon Faithfull, *REEF*, 2014, Photography by Gavin Weber

'There indeed under my eyes, ruined, destroyed, lay a town, its roofs open to the sky, its temples fallen, its arches dislocated, its columns lying on the ground, from which one could still recognise the massive character of Tuscan architecture.'

Video still from '*44*' DVD, 44 min, 2005

Video still from *EZY1899: Reenactment for a Future Scenario*,
HD video, 12 min, 2012

Thus Jules Verne in *20,000 Leagues Under the Sea* (1870) described the sort of sunken dreamworld that had long been a common motif in myth and literature but which took on a rich, strange new life in the latter half of the 19th century. In Verne's fantastical fiction, in popular science periodicals and in the precincts of the new natural history museums, the Victorian public discovered the baroque geology of the ocean bed and the teeming creatures that lived there. With this curiosity about marine life and its setting came an odd fantasy: the idea that one might live at the bottom of the sea, surrounded by alien beings and among ruins or wreckage from the world above.

It was a notion stimulated by the image of Verne's Captain Nemo and crew walking around on the sea bed, by illustrations showing aquatic flora and fauna published by naturalists such as Philip Henry Gosse, by the craze for domestic aquariums that Gosse's books and magazines helped to create. Suddenly it was possible to project oneself imaginatively onto the ocean floor, which had until then been a terrifying void, home to unspeakable horrors, among them the bones of the drowned and the rotting hulks of sunken ships. For a time—the craze was actually at its height before Verne's novel, in the 1860s—bourgeois domestic life could be carried on in constant proximity to reminders of this watery realm: vitrines filled with fish, molluscs, crustaceans, underwater forests of plant life and carefully wrought miniature shipwrecks or drowned columns from mock-classical ruins.

Simon Faithfull's *REEF* involves, for sure, a more sober view of the sea bed. But there is still something about it of the Victorians' urge to overcome the distance between the domestic interior and the depths of the ocean, to somehow inhabit mundane and fantastic worlds at the same time—and also to see the forms and processes of the deep as sculptural, to think of nature itself as an artist. Several of Faithfull's previous projects have seen him invoke these desires, though not without comedy. In his video *Going Nowhere* (2011), a figure in jeans and a white shirt—it's the artist himself—walks about on the sea bed, apparently without any breathing apparatus, as if he were wandering on the sea shore and not ten metres below the surface of the Adriatic. As we'll see, this sort of incongruity is everywhere in Faithfull's work; but, for now, it's enough to note that one of his recurring gestures is this positioning of the everyday at the edges not only of knowledge or culture but of physical plausibility.

Simon Faithfull, *REEF*, 2014, Photography by Gavin Weber

At the time of writing, *REEF* is still a matter of plans and projections, Faithfull having to trust to logistics, technology, environmental conditions and the many collaborators without whom the project would be impossible. The work involves towing a boat—a ferro-cement hull at the end of its useful life, cleaned and prepared according to regulations set down by the Marine Management Oorganisation—out from the coast at Weymouth, where it will be set on fire and then sunk. (Fire has played a part in the artist's work before: his 2012 video *EZY1899: Reenactment for a Future Scenario* sees him silver-suited inside a plane-like structure used to simulate aircraft fires.) The 'sinking event', as Faithfull calls it, will be subject to an array of observations and recordings. Five cameras on the boat itself, powered by wind turbine and solar panel, are to be linked to a buoy that will remain floating above the eventual wreck. Another camera will record the event from a nearby ship, and a seventh from cliffs overlooking the scene. The onboard cameras will continue to transmit from underwater; the others will stop when the sea is calm and empty, and night falls. *REEF* will be exhibited at Fabrica in October 2014 as part of Brighton Photo Biennial, the footage of the sinking to be shown on two large screens, while five smaller monitors transmit live from the bottom of the sea.

Two timescales then, at least: the sinking event itself and its protracted aftermath. If *REEF* is a collaboration on the surface—with maritime authorities, a marine biologist at University College London and the harbour master at Whitstable in Kent, from whom Faithfull sought advice—

it will also be a collaboration with the sea itself, or rather with the algae, barnacles and other organisms that will slowly begin to colonise the wreck. It is common now as part of the management of marine environments to sink artificial reefs in the form of old boats or even railway carriages, which form habitats for all manner of living things, from the flora that attaches itself to a wreck to the creatures that hide within or around it. The live camera feed to the sunken boat will continue until 2017. Faithfull's *REEF* will not be a finished sculpture, nor the mere residue of an event or performance, however spectacular, but an artefact that will go on making itself, encrusting and elaborating itself, for years.

In that sense, the project takes its place among several of Faithfull's works that have to do with entropy and environment, with a certain kind of productive or generative failure. There are the obvious instances of destruction, of literal overreaching, such as the fate of a domestic chair sent by balloon to the edge of space in *Escape Vehicle no.6* (2004). Or his failed journey into the Arctic Circle in Finland to witness the northern lights, resulting in the two-screen video piece *Aurora Borealis (Unseen)* (2008). There have been more ambiguous journeys, however. In the course of a two-month trip to Antarctica in 2004–05, Faithfull made a number of works that both acknowledge the alien sublimity of the seas and territory into which he was heading and, at the same time, record his own, or the environment's, failure to live up to that natural and aesthetic extremity. *En route*, Faithfull filmed the sea and ice through the porthole of his cabin: a partial, sequestered view that appears in *'44'* (2006). In Antarctica itself, he visited Stromness, the whaling station reached by Ernest Shackleton's stranded exploration party in 1916: in Faithfull's film the place is a ghost town, a ruin frequented only by seals.

There is, then, a bathos attached to Faithfull's physical and imaginative excursions: the work sets up expectations of spectacle or sublimity only to dash them with a deadpan sort of conceptual slapstick. This may be the case with *REEF* too: the drama of the burning boat declining to muddy footage as the sunken hull does very little indeed, or apparently so, given the slowness of the natural processes to which it's about to be subject. Except of course that it will have become a new environment, a reminder of actual reefs under threat elsewhere, and an oblique reminder too that the very concept of environment owes its development, in scientific terms, to the period in the 19th century when artificial (including underwater) worlds were the rage: from the domestic aquarium to the Crystal Palace. Faithfull's *REEF* will be an artificial environment inserted into the natural. Or will it—considering how much it is hedged about with historical precursors, present significance and artistic machinery—be the other way round?

Migrant Images

TJ
DEMOS

in
conversation
with

BEN
BURBRIDGE

Still from *Otolith II*, 2007, by the Otolith Group.
Courtesy of the Otolith Group

Ben Burbridge: You have made an important contribution to discussions around politics and documentary. Could you say something about the ways you have framed relationships between documentary, representation, statelessness and citizenship?

TJ Demos: For me, this problematisation of representation has been key to thinking through photographic practices, such as Ahlam Shibli's, which I address in my recent book *The Migrant Image*. As the title indicates, the book attempts to take account of the mobility and thus slipperiness of the image, especially in this age of the increasingly dominant experience of media displacement, of traveling images, of continually reframed, reprocessed, recontextualised digital forms. Yet it also addresses photographic ontology, which Shibli's work addresses in a way that brings together forms of political and aesthetic statelessness. Consider her series *Unrecognized* (2000), which portrays Palestinians of Bedouin descent who have been relegated by the State of Israel to the position of legal non-recognition, as they refuse to be moved to recognised settlements from the lands they have called home for generations (consequently they are denied permanent infrastructure, electricity and education, and have faced a brutal policy of forced relocation in recent years). What's so provocative about Shibli's photography

is how she engages the complexity of attempting to represent the unrepresented, yet doing so without re-fixing her subjects in a subsequent position of static objecthood, for instance, as the depoliticised object of humanitarian concern and protection, devoid of the potentiality of political subjectivity that her photography generates. In this sense, the visual obfuscations and blockages that frequently materialise in her photographs act as negations of any sovereign knowledge viewers might presume to bring to, or find in, the images, which do double work in allegorising the very necropolitical fragmentation that governs their lives.

I've also been motivated in my writing to extend the discussion of the politics of photography into the expanded field of moving image practices, which similarly exceed, and are even frequently opposed to, 'representation'. This is quite clear in video, with its multiplicity of relations within and between images. I'm thinking, for instance, of the Otolith Group's films, especially their *Otolith Trilogy*, which sparks the potentialising of the past, opening up what these artists (Kodwo Eshun and Anjalika Sagar) term 'past potential futures', dreams of prospective liberation embedded in the media of former ages since repressed, remaining as yet unfulfilled but ever capable also of being newly unlocked and redirected in the present. For me this offers one approximation of the political ontology of the photographic and filmic image, defining a powerful idea and an emancipating project. >

Still from *Otolith III*, 2009, by the Otolith Group.
Courtesy of the Otolith Group

Derrida's *Specters of Marx* offers a useful instrument of analysis that insists on the archive's foundational relation to institutionalisation and power, knowledge of which can precisely undermine sovereignty. Consider Sven Augustijnen's *Spectres*, a film that investigates the archive surrounding Belgian's relation to its former colonial possession, the Congo, and explores the way that archives may officially act to seal world historical events (for instance, that of the Belgium-directed murder of Patrice Lumumba) safely within official narratives, but which may also reveal the aesthetic traces of repression as well as defence mechanisms that form so many ghosts that hover around the memories of that past. Augustijnen's film is remarkable for potentialising the image in order to rescue its emancipatory energies, discovering in the archive a demand for justice that has gone unfulfilled for so many years. That past of an unfulfilled decolonisation, for Augustijnen, might be also said to be discovered in the stateless elements of the archive, unmoored aesthetically and delinked from national sovereignty, and his film invites viewers to take up a new relation to Belgium's colonial and neocolonial relation to the DRC. For me, Derrida's book was critically enabling in helping to articulate the spectro-poetics of this film, and to consider what I think is the film's great ambition: to learn to live with ghosts, more justly.

BB: Where else do issues of collaboration feature in your work? I am particularly interested in your current interest in art and ecology.

TJD: I'm interested in considering collaboration especially where, in its progressive guise, it offers ways of breaking down divisions and hierarchies, as with the production and reception of cultural forms, which is important to a new ecology of politics as much as a politics of ecology. One example where media figures prominently in such a practice is *The Sovereign Forest*, a project of the Indian artist Amar Kanwar, particularly as its installation appears at the Samadrusti Campus in Bhubaneswar, Orissa. There, corporate mining interests coupled with a militarised police force have threatened environmental destruction and the social displacement of tribals and villagers from their traditional lands. Kanwar's mixed-media installation figures as an integral part of the Samadrusti's community centre, educational institution, Odia-language independent newspaper publisher, and video editing platform. As such, it offers a grassroots site of inclusive, collective reception for Kanwar's activities and mixed-media installation, which, among its elements, comprises a living archive of corporate and state crimes against the local people and environment, and a presentation of a rice seed bank, dramatising the possibilities of the return to non-commodifiable organic agriculture as a way to re-establish a commons for the reproduction of life (resonating with projects like Vandana Shiva's).

Samadrusti also provides training in video production and editing, where villagers and tribals, who have had no access to such media in the past, can gain technological know-how and assistance in creating documentary accounts of their struggle and in getting those accounts disseminated through the institution's network. The aim is to contest the generally pro-corporate views of mainstream media that dominate India's mediascape and control the narrative in Orissa's regional news services. Kanwar's project is thus one element in a wider structure of participation that defies a long-term, locally based platform for non-corporate media in Orissa, wherein collaboration plays a central role, for it challenges the divisions between top-down-thinking government elites, corporate technocrats, compromised mass media journalists and anti-democratic financial interests, on the one hand, and on the other, the voices of subsistence farmers, non-violent activists and indigenous communities. >

Still from *Otolith II*, 2007, by the Otolith Group.
Courtesy of the Otolith Group

As a result of providing this platform, the traditionally excluded and disenfranchised can air grievances against corporate and state human and civil rights abuses, and gain a voice in the collective determination of land-use policy and the meaning of 'development' in this region—whether it is the technological exploitation of the environment for the benefit of the few or the spiritual–cultural sustainability of traditional forms of life practised by Orissa's tribals for generations. As such, collaboration defines a collective form of political solidarity and participation in a mass movement of non-partisan politics (avoiding the false choice between state-sanctioned neoliberalism and Naxalite-armed insurrection), where artistic practice, at least in Kanwar's model, generates social connection and institutional support.

> **BB: At the end of *The Migrant Image* you seem to identify links between your work and aspects of the Occupy movement; an interest developed further in the special issue of *Third Text* you edited last year. Could you say something about your interest, and the links you have identified between the movement and your work?**

TJD: For me, the greatest transformative possibilities for political change exist with social movements, and one important question for politically engaged artistic practice then becomes how to diversify audiences and participants beyond the siloed fields of specialisation presented in art galleries, academic disciplines and large-scale exhibitions. How can we challenge such boundaries and cultivate progressive transversal movements that can create solidarities between those in the cultural domain and others in activist social movements? Recent examples unfortunately demonstrate mostly missed opportunities for this sort of interaction: consider large-scale exhibitions such as the 13th Istanbul Biennial directed by curator Fulya Erdemci that coincided with the occupation of Taksim Gezi Park and its brutal suppression by Turkey's Prime Minister Erdogan. While in the run-up to the show Erdemci expressed the wish to engage with the spatial politics of the rapidly gentrifying city and its anti-democratic governance, the Gezi uprising had the effect of pushing her biennial back into the show's largely privatised gallery sites, while the exhibition neglected to reach out to activists and the occupation to develop forms of political solidarity and communication, perhaps out of fear of alienating its corporate sponsors.

Another example is the visit to the US Social Forum in Detroit initiated by the New York-based 16beaver group at the invitation of AND AND AND as a part of dOCUMENTA (13), in 2010, in order to generate an open debate concerning the role of art in the development of social movements, and the potential collaboration between cultural and artistic work, institutions and political struggle.[1] Linked activities included participation in the Allied Media Conference, a platform for creative media solutions to building solidarity and practising social justice, and a research workshop on contemporary social movements, drawing together a diversity of social actors, such as grassroots activists, unions members and non-governmental organisations, policy experts, students, intellectuals, journalists and artists, to consider transnational alliances and local movement-building to strengthen the new global left. While those activities included some live web-based streaming of events, there has been little online archiving of recordings, which points to the ongoing challenge of how to maximise media access so that such discussions and networking don't terminate in local, face-to-face encounters.

Finally, there remains catalytic energy after Occupy that emerged in that movement, such as the activities of the BDS Arts Coalition—dedicated to the Boycotts, Divestment and Sanctions movement against Israel in view of its violation of Palestinian rights—which has recently challenged the appearance of Creative Time's *Living as Form* exhibition at The Technion in Haifa, a university with extensive research-and-development connections to the Israeli military and defence technology industry. The campaign has involved local organising in New York, as well as a high-visibility media drive to expose the contradictions involved in this exhibition project, one dedicated to progressive and political forms of social practice, violating the terms of BDS and implicitly endorsing an Israeli institution bearing a 'central role in maintaining the unjust and illegal occupation of Palestine'.[2] It remains imperative to build forms of civic democratic participation from within and beyond the cultural domain, in order to maintain pressure on such organisations as Creative Time that risk collapsing into accommodation, as well as, more broadly, to generate collective political agency in the shared determination of new forms of decolonised life. >

Still from *Otolith II*, 2007, by the Otolith Group.
Courtesy of the Otolith Group

Still from *Otolith II*, 2007, by the Otolith Group.
Courtesy of the Otolith Group

13th Istanbul Biennial, 2013

BB: Much has been made of the supposed democratisation of news-making and the media in recent years, with emphasis often placed on roles played by new technologies. What do you make of these suggestions? And do they impact on your work?

TJD: This question's positive ring seems to speak to the already outmoded narratives of techno-utopia surrounding the events of the Arab Spring, relating to the hyped culture of mobile phone cameras, citizen journalism and Facebook–Twitter revolutions, which of course went hand-in-hand with corporate IT expansion, entrepreneurial neoliberalism and state-manipulated social media, surveillance and techno-control. The result has been a post-revolution era defined less by the democratic potential of media and more by a hermeneutics of suspicion, which plays into the hands of nation-state domination and anti-hegemonic challenges alike. Still, one can't underestimate the significance of the growth of non-corporate news sources in recent years—such as *Democracy Now!, Truthout, Common Dreams* and *Red Pepper*, to mention only a few leading independent media organisations—in providing alternative accounts to mainstream news, which represent little more than the conservative face of corporate–governmental power. Even so, it takes time to engage with these independent sources (time that many people don't have), and these counter-sites of production and distribution, while they hopefully are continuing to grow, figure as only a drop in the bucket against the mega-funded media enterprises they're up against. More than the positive democratisation of news-making and media, critics and commentators in the last few years have been increasingly attentive to media surveillance and the boundless reach of national security, especially with the revelations of the governmental

spying campaigns of Julian Assange's Wikileaks, Edward Snowden's exposure of the NSA's and GCHQ's hacking and data-mining activities and Aaron Swartz's tragic attempt to open access to commodified and protected information archives. While these may be only the most spectacular of cases that show the systematic isolation, criminalisation and banishment that happens when citizens and activists attempt to access media systems and privatised information archives, they do dramatise the fact that media technology is a central instrument of state power, one whose exclusive operating rights it will go to extraordinary lengths to protect. Nonetheless, media defines an ever crucial site of contest between the forces of corporate consumerism and governmental control, and those fighting for equality, inclusive participation, and human and civil rights—perhaps more so than most art institutions.

Occupy LSX, 5 November 2011. © Haydn

Occupy Gezi NYC, 15 June 2013. © Michael Fleshman

1   16beaver group, 'Participating in Detroit',   2   Mostafa Heddaya, 'Over 100 artists   http://hyperallergic.com/131497/over-
     www.16beavergroup.org/anotherworld/   and intellectuals call for withdrawal   100-artists-and-intellectuals-call-for-
     detroit.htm (10 July 2014).   from Creative Time exhibition',   withdrawal-from-creative-time-exhibition/
                                                            Hyperallergic Forum,   (10 June 2014).

Amore e Piombo:
The Photography of
Extremes in 1970s Italy

Anti-nuclear protest, c. 1970s. © TEAM Editorial Services/Alinari

Roger Hargreaves
& Federica Chiocchetti

Pier Paolo Pasolini, Ninetto Davoli and Franco Citti, c. 1970s.
© TEAM Editorial Services/Alinari

The rise of the Italian Communist Party during the 1970s acted as catalyst for a period of instability and intense political violence. Roger Hargreaves and Federica Chiocchetti explore this complex time in Italian history via an extraordinary moment in Italian photojournalism.

> Through me you go into a city of weeping;
> through me you go into eternal pain; through
> me you go amongst the lost people.

Dante Alighieri, *The Inferno*

Forty years on and Italy's 'Years of Lead' are still shrouded in mystery. Philip Willan in his book, *Puppetmasters: The Political Use of Terrorism in Italy*, records that, 'in this period of domestic terrorism 365 people were killed and more than 1,000 wounded'.[1] The number of terrorist incidents, from unexploded letter bombs to kneecappings, kidnappings and mass killings, ran into the thousands, reaching a peak of activity in the years 1977–79.

What is widely accepted is that the catalyst for the so-called 'Strategy of Tension' was the rise of the Italian Communist Party as an electoral force. For the far left, the Party's willingness to reach a *historic* political *compromise* with the Christian Democrats represented a betrayal of principles. Externally, the Soviet Union was less than keen on a democratic model of communism. Equally, the USA could not countenance a Communist Party as a coalition partner within the government of a NATO ally. At the dark heart of things were the murkier manoeuvrings of clandestine groups within NATO, the CIA, the multiple branches of the Italian secret services and the P2 (Propaganda Due) Masonic Lodge: their collective strategy, to foster right-wing terroristic outrages masquerading as acts of left-wing radicalism.

While the neo-fascist Black Brigades perpetrated indiscriminate acts of violence against the public at large, the Red Brigades favoured the selective targeting of specific industrialists, politicians and public officials. In this state of emergency, 'anti-terrorism' measures were rapidly introduced to destabilise the Left, while the state acted as an 'impartial' mediator between 'opposing extremisms'. It was a policy guided in part by the mantra of Prince Salina, in Tomasi di Lampedusa's *The Leopard*: 'Everything needs to change, so everything can stay the same.'[2]

Despite countless attempts to unravel the political chaos of the times, key tragic events—from the Piazza Fontana bombing in Milan in 1969 to Aldo Moro's kidnap and assassination by the Red Brigades in Rome in 1978—remain unresolved. Far from offering answers, the BPB14 exhibition *Amore e Piombo* seeks to concoct a viscous minestrone from the ingredients of the season: gnostic terrorism, coalition government, conspiracy and collaboration. It's a dish that is peppered with an Italian twist on style and salted with industrial unrest, triggered by the economic stagnation of the OPEC oil crisis that brought Europe's fiercest and most radical working class movements to the street. To the mix should be added a widening split between an increasingly secular society and the Catholic traditions of family, as debates surfaced on the issues of divorce and abortion. >

Rome, in common with Paris, London and Prague, had witnessed its revolutionary rattling of 1968. The Italian Autonomist student movement, which proposed direct action and sparked occupations of universities and factories in 1967 and 1968, escalated into the so-called 'hot autumn' of industrial action in 1969. At the height of the tensions, a bomb exploded in Piazza Fontana in Milan: 17 people were killed and 88 injured.

The 'Season of Lead' (*Anni di Piombo*) had begun. The trails that flow from the bombing mark the complex weave of conspiracy and counter-conspiracy, reprisal and retribution that characterised Italy in the 1970s. Many lines of investigations were initially pursued, the first of which placed the blame on anarchists. The dancer Pietro Valpreda emerged as the chief suspect. He was jailed without trial until 1972, to be finally cleared in 1981. Around 80 anarchists were initially brought in for questioning, including Giuseppe Pinelli, a railway worker in his forties, who helpfully rode on a scooter to the Milan police station, as there was no room in the van. Pinelli fell to his death from a fourth floor window shortly after chief police inspector Luigi Calabresi had temporarily left the room during a break from the interrogations. The story became the material for Dario Fo's play *Accidental Death of an Anarchist*, in which the fool sardonically quips that 'Scandals are the fertiliser of Western democracy… out of the indignation comes a burp. A liberating burp. It's like Alka-Seltzer. But nothing changes.'[3] The first official version of Pinelli's death was 'suicide'. Later, in 1975, it was attributed to an 'active illness'. Both causes were greeted with astonishment and ridicule, with the Piazza Fontana saga reaching its surreal climax when a dummy representing Pinelli was thrown out of the window to re-enact the mysterious fall for the benefit of assembled photographers, among them a young Massimo Vitali.

To add to the atmosphere of terror in 1972, Calabresi was assassinated. This was the prelude for what John Foot in his book *Italy's Divided Memory* describes as the 'post-Piazza Fontana period, marked by conflicts over all forms of memory, including plaques, memorials, and monuments'.[4] A bust of Calabresi was duly unveiled at the Milan Police Headquarters at a ceremony attended by the Interior Minister, Mariano Rumor. Moments after Rumor left, Gianfranco Bertoli threw a hand grenade at the remaining dignitaries. A policeman kicked it away into a crowd of on-lookers, killing four and injuring 45. It later emerged that Bertoli, a supposed anarchist, was a secret service informant with links to Gladio, the clandestine NATO operation in Europe.

As investigations into the original Piazza Fontana bombing continued, a more troubling and complex explanation emerged: that this was the work of neo-fascist extremists with established links to the State Secret Service (SID) possibly aided by the helpful advice of the Greek Colonels in preparation for a coup d'état. In the intervening years, eight separate trials and inquiries have failed to reach a consensus on the true architects of the atrocity.

Collaboration, or its lack, in Italian politics is taken so *seriously* that it often degenerates into corruption and collusion with criminal organisations. A painfully slow and fallacious justice does the rest. The expression the 'Italian job' exists to indicate the tortuous workings under the table. Terrorism, during the 'long decade of the short century', was not immune from these convoluted logics of intrigue. Paradoxically, the more knowledge that has been acquired on both Piazza Fontana and the Moro affair, the less a consensus has been reached.

Perhaps one can better grasp the complexity of those burning years in the stories of Sicilian writer Leonardo Sciascia. He described his early 1970s masterpiece *Equal Danger* as 'a fable about power that, in the impenetrable form of a concatenation that we can roughly term *mafioso*, works steadily greater degradation'.[5] Elio Petri adapted Sciascia's *One Way or Another* into a 1976 film that offered a dystopian premonition of things to come. A series of murders disturb a spiritual retreat of the Christian Democrats, in which Gian Maria Volonté plays Aldo Moro. The Moro character tries to solve the mystery behind the killings of the Christian Democrats by combining parts of companies' acronyms to which the victims had illegally belonged. Somewhat disturbingly, the fictional Moro is killed two years before his actual murder in 1978.

The nature of conspiracy is its secrecy. There are no paper trails, just whispers in the deep shadows. Events such as the Piazza Fontana bombing were planned to cause maximum outrage: spectaculars that would be replayed on the evening news and splashed across the papers and magazines. Reportage, and with it a distinctly Italian style of photojournalism, would emerge as an unwitting ally in the strategic fermentation of 'tension'. >

Conscientious objector protest, c. 1970s.
© TEAM Editorial Services/Alinari

Police against extreme left protesters, Rome, October 1977.
© TEAM Editorial Services/Alinari

Italian Press photography has been indelibly stamped with the brand of Fellini's seminal film of 1960, *La Dolce Vita*. In the period between the 1950s and the 1960s, paparazzi photographers such as Tazio Secchiaroli and Elio Sorci manufactured an alluring and enduring catalogue of images that made mischievous play between intrusion and collusion as they stalked the back-lots of Cinecittà and the cafés of via Veneto. Yet the tabloid style of confrontational, high-contrast images that exposed their subjects to the bright light of day and the harsh flash of night dates back much further. Adolfo Porry-Pastore is widely regarded as the father of modern Italian paparazzi. In 1919 he established his own agency, VEDO, Visioni Editoriali Diffuse Ovunque (Editorial Visions Spread Everywhere), to distribute his own style of competitive, abrasive, conniving photography that matched his refined palate for scandal and confrontation.

Tazio Secchiaroli found his first job working for VEDO in 1952. What changed for Sechiaroli's generation was the late 1950s boom in the Italian film industry. Cheap labour, government subsidies and a Mediterranean climate made Rome an attractive alternative to the spiralling costs of film production in Hollywood. Ever bigger films with more glittering stars were drawn to Italy. The 1963 movie *Cleopatra* not only threw Elizabeth Taylor into the arms of Richard Burton but also consumed 400 miles of steel scaffolding that created a two-year steel shortage in the Italian construction industry. A secondary industry of Paparazzi photographers emerged. A camera, a flash, a Lambretta and an attitude were the prerequisites for work supplying the growing number of small agencies that fed the voracious appetite of an international editorial market with a taste for all things celebrity and Italian.

'Of course,' wrote Secchiaroli, 'we too would like to stroll through an evening, have a cup of coffee in blissful peace, and see via Veneto as a splendid international promenade, rather than one big workplace, or even a theatre of war.'[6] When Italy descended into near civil war in the 1970s, the photographers were on hand, trained, armed, with their supply lines in place and ready to roll. >

Pino Pelosi, self-confessed killer of Pier Paolo Pasolini, Rome, 2 February 1976.
© TEAM Editorial Services/Alinari

Arguably the most traumatic and climactic event of the 'season' was the kidnap and murder of former Prime Minister Aldo Moro. The photography of staged events would serve to punctuate the narrative. On the morning of 16 March 1978, *en route* to Parliament, Moro was kidnapped. His driver and security detail were machine- gunned. All five died at the scene. Moro was spirited away.

The aftermath of shattered car windows, strewn bodies, priests administering last rights, police and press generated graphic and almost cinematic imagery that erupted across the world's press. For 55 days Moro was held captive. Four days into captivity a Polaroid photograph was released along with a series of communiqués of Moro crouched beneath a Red Brigades flag holding a copy of the previous day's *La Repubblica* newspaper. The singular photograph was copied into black and white and wired across the world.

While negotiations continued with the periodic release of letters from Moro, the police and secret services conducted a highly public and sometimes knowingly fruitless search. A thousand battle-clad soldiers placed Rome in virtual lockdown. The name 'Gradoli' emerged through intelligence. Rather than search the via Gradoli, the site of a key Red Brigade hideout, later discovered to be littered with clues, the authorities headed to the seaside resort of Gradoli. Further hunts were conducted in the frozen mountain lake Duchessa, 70 miles north-east of Rome. Holes were dynamited in the icy cover and a quarry drained. It made for compelling press imagery conveying the illusion of an exhaustive hunt. >

Brigitte Bardot, Rome, c. 1970s.
© TEAM Editorial Services/Alinari

Aldo Moro's kidnap, via Fani, Rome, 16 March 1978.
© TEAM Editorial Services/Alinari

Giulio Andreotti, c. 1970s.
© TEAM Editorial Services/Alinari

On 9 May, following a phone call to Moro's assistant,
Francesco Tritto, the politician's bullet-ridden body
was discovered in the boot of a red Renault 4 parked
in central Rome. One photojournalist, Gianni Giansanti,
witnessed the discovery before the police cordoned off
the area. His pictures were syndicated around the world.

The photojournalism of the period colludes to
create a back catalogue of imagery of what happened
without ever revealing who made it happen and why.
Rather than offering a definitive truth, it serves to present
photography as a provider of fragments of admissible
evidence. Italy is a country of extreme and tragicomic
contradictions where the concepts of truth and justice
are 'creatively' interpreted, and where a deep and bourgeois sense of forgiving infused with a Catholic absolution
of guilt reigns supreme.

1   Philip Willan, *Puppetmasters: The Political
    Use of Terrorism in Italy* (Lincoln, NE:
    iUniverse, 2002), p. 17.

2   Giuseppe Tomasi di Lampedusa, *The
    Leopard*, trans. Archibald Colquhoun
    (London: Vintage Classics, 2007), p. 19.

3   Dario Fo, *Accidental Death of an Anarchist*,
    trans. Ed Emery (London: Methuen
    Books, 1992).

4   John Foot, *Italy's Divided Memory* (New
    York: Palgrave Macmillan, 2009), p. 185.

5   Leonardo Sciascia, *Equal Danger*, trans.
    Adrienne Foulke (New York: New York
    Review of Books, 2003), p. 119.

6   Tazio Secchiaroli, *Greatest of the Paparazzi,
    Diego Mormorio* (New York, Abrams, 1999), p. 23.

This Man Sits Alone: Some Thoughts on Photography and Collaboration

Daniel C. Blight

Earlier in the year, Photoworks put out a call for submissions of new work relating to the theme of 'collaboration'. Writer and curator Daniel C. Blight offers his thoughts on the six projects we have selected to feature from more than 200 submitted.

Alice Myers, from the series *Nothing is Impossible Under the Sun*, 2014

What follows sits somewhere between an essay (taken here as an attempt or effort at something), and fiction (the act of inventing characters and situations). It tries to offer some insights into the meanings of collaboration through the study of a number of photographs made collaboratively. It moves from Calais to Syria, Cairo to New York, and then into Sir Benjamin Stone's archive and the subway stations of Dusseldorf, grasping at some of the ways of working and thinking that inform collaborative photographic practices. The writing moves around a selection of photographs to create a series of reflections, statements and descriptions of the objects, characters and themes they contain or suggest. I have tried to describe other people's collaborations while, at the same time, attempting to produce collaborations of my own, writing *with* a number of disparate and often unrelated images.

Above and Overleaf: Alice Myers, from the series
Nothing is Impossible Under the Sun, 2014

Alice Myers

Look at my face, eye, head, nose and my hair. Remind yourself of me. A collaboration if I choose to look. Your body: a reminder of you. To lessen the burden of loneliness. Because we respect each other's work. The reason that more than one human exists is to provide help and support to those that are lost in their efforts to collaborate. The coupling of things, the tripling of subjects, the mess of companionship. Intellectual, intuitive, emotional and emphatic. This is political, and no one should be excluded.

perfer
disappear
poverty
Nervous
Target
Task
Deputy
Effort
fair
un fair
Differ
Attempt
Torture

Above and Overleaf: Alice Myers, from the series
Nothing is Impossible Under the Sun, 2014

I am a technically an illegal subject. I am a body of uninvited knowledge.

The port of Calais—distinct from the town of Calais Nord—is a drab ferry terminal on the Northern coast of France. Facing the English Channel, it is 21 miles from the White Cliffs of Dover, and steeped in colonial history. Run as a major trade port by the English, it was reclaimed by the French in the 1550s. A Napoleonic army once stood there with plans to invade England. So did the Germans 140 years later.

As an English national, I use Calais to go on 'cultural holidays', moving quickly on towards places such as Paris or Arles. I move with ease because I hold a British passport. The history of my privilege is embedded between the pages of that little red book: the meaningless legacy of something I don't believe in; documentary evidence of my *right to enter* other nations.

It is not everyone who possesses this status. Nor does everyone share my beliefs. But they should have the right to move and find work, sanctuary, rest. The people who reside in Calais' makeshift homes, squats and refugee camps are persecuted because of their nationality or, sometimes, because of their beliefs. Due to a farcical series of social policies regarding the status of one human being over another, certain individual's rights have been withdrawn.

In a video on Alice Myers's website, a man called Abdul breathes on the camera's lens. It is testament to his legitimate presence. There is energy in his refugee community, a sense of sharing that is not recognised by the European border authorities. Where equality is refused, it grows instead under the surface, out of sight, between the lining of canvas or on the foam of the English Channel. >

Rancière Reading Group

Look at Leonardo DiCaprio. His hair is swept to one side, as if a gust of wind had stopped above his head, freezing his barnet as though a Brylcreem icon. He is holding a swan, a symbol of monogamy and fidelity.

We are the spectators. He switches roles and we absorb him, passively. He blends obnoxiousness with confidence, dusted with a boyish and knowing self-deprecation. His sensitivity is a bullshit swan.

In a Rococo-style painting a swan investigates the opening of a woman's vagina. The work is attributed to the well-known 18th-century artist François Boucher.

How can we collaborate when this kind of theatre prohibits action? Ask Jaques Rancière. A reading group in Cairo interprets his propositions. Various images—disparate and expansive like the philosopher's references —are brought into use by a community of practitioners. Rancière invites us to depart from his words, which he reminds us are *only* words, offering instead a space to narrate and translate. I want to talk, clearly and directly, about a few of the images the group have shared.

As a sequence, the work becomes its own performance. The art world has said more than enough about Rancière and *The Emancipated Spectator*.

The flowers were brought from a friend's house outside Cairo. This valley by the Nile has a favourable climate for growing flowers. You can clip them with a fingernail because the stems split easily.

Nadia's auntie had three children, and we were asked to look after them for the afternoon. We decided to write a short play and entertain them in that tried and tested manner. She approved. Children respond to humour but also to things that don't make sense. You can offer a child confusion, and they will laugh at it with you. You can offer a child a photograph, and they will tell you what it is.

No-one quite guessed at first. There was a sort of preamble in the kitchen and then we showed the children a selection of photographs we'd found on the internet, loosely inspired by Egyptian surrealism, among other things.

No story is complete until a reference to an animal has been made, we told them.

'What is the internet?'

'A place for all the lost things', said one of the children.

'OK, what can you find there?'

'Pictures of animals and pictures of things—cats, dogs, famous people.'

We wanted the children to understand how images can tell stories and that stories are made to be completed by active participants. It takes at least two people to imagine something unique. A series of pictures; something beyond seeing without thinking or speaking or moving. We strengthen ideas, removing the anxiety of working alone. I can only be alone when I write, and it is from that place that I create a kind of fiction. Stultifying to some, but it seems as natural as pictures and animals and sofas to me.

Rancière described contemporary art in terms of three types of stultification: among them, the way in which roles are switched and exchanged in the creation of artworks. He refers to the treatment of photographs as paintings and the phenomenon of theatre without speech. He invites the passivity of spectatorship to open up to activity. This is a place where images can change the meaning of the world. >

Anders Birger

How many of these tables could one get on Twitter?
I could zoom and crop each one individually, uploading
a pixel-reduced extraction to social media. Six tweets
of six tables; six re-tweets of six tweets of six tables.
This act would offer a *version* of this image to an audience
that is potentially huge. This is how a scene is reproduced and manipulated in network culture. We're
collaborating with the technology of communication,
but also of big data, business, capital.

   Violence in Syria undergoes a similar process.
We have to be clear about what we see in the frame
of social media, and the reality of what is happening,
politically and culturally, that which few of us will
ever know or witness first hand. We're all talking but
very few of us *know*. One-hundred and forty characters
on Twitter, nothing IRL.

Anders Birger, from the series *This Damn Weather*, 2012

This man sits alone. He evokes loneliness and loss, even if he isn't, actually, lonely. We empathise because our intuition tells us to do so. We give this man the benefit of support *in case* he has lost someone. Photographs manipulate. This table can't be cropped because it has a person sitting behind it. Who would do such a thing? This is a loss to the whole of humanity. A reflection of what we have all lost by allowing a minority to undertake the majority of the suffering. War is a kind of theatre. We are all participants. We could say no, but we stay silent. It is a theatre without speech.

Look in these mirrors. You're not looking at yourself (for once). Two men pace the street, captured by a carefully positioned camera. The positioning of the camera is key to taking a good photograph. Photograph to learn something. This photographer focuses on the quiet points of thought and meditation that exist in conflict zones. There is the action and then there are the people that are living around it, continuing their daily lives. For every footstep, 100 of the wrong tweets are shared. These are the tweets that abstract the reality of the situation in Syria. Speak of the ego of the West more than the crisis in the East. >

Anders Birger, from the series *This Damn Weather*, 2012

Sophie Rickett
and Bettina von Zwehl

Some things that are left out:

The meat trimmings after a roast dinner; those mussels that remain closed; odd socks; a redundant clause; a contentious point; a multiple exposure; the photograph that happened twice and was better the first time; parts of an archive that aren't interpreted or described; the albino child; the black child; the school bully as he or she realises the error of their ways and recedes into social isolation; the Christmas tree dried out and discarded; a ghost note; the takeaway coffee I assumed you might want before our meeting but was politely declined; a spare wheel (actually and metaphorically).

Wednesday 21 November 1906:

> Took some photographs in my room at the Hotel of old deeds of the Calthorpes.
>
> Had lunch at the Hotel and then went to the British Museum to see Dr. Budge and Mr. King. Took them some photographs.
>
> To the House of Commons at 4.0.
>
> At 9.0 went to Sir Norman Lockyer's party at Earl's Court. Met there Sir David Gill (of the Cape Observatory), Mr Fowler and many other men of the scientific world.
>
> Home at 12.0.[1]

So writes Sir Benjamin Stone, the conservative politician and prolific amateur photographer. The short diary entry alludes to the importance of physical description and memory. We can only imagine the spaces in between these lines: the descriptions of the objects contained in his room as he photographed the old deeds, or the smell of Earl's Court at the time of the party. Why leave so much out?

Sophy Rickett and Bettina von Zwehl want to interrogate the Benjamin Stone archive. They have focused on a missing page from the section that Stone labelled 'miscellaneous'. This 'chance encounter', as the two photographers put it, allowed them to consider their own production as artists and the things that have been left behind in the display and publishing of their work. Stone's miscellany and the collaborators' own work are conflated. It is the form of Stone's pages, rather than the content of his photographs, that is recreated here.

Perhaps collaboration can be seen as the term we give to the archive of human relationships? Such an act requires us to create something; to document the existence of mutual thought.

---

a. Sophy Rickett and Bettina von Zwehl, *Album 31*, 2013. Centrepiece: X-ray composite of BvZ's hands (obere Extremitäten), 4th August, 2010 at 15:25, Radiologie am Herkommerplatz, Munich. Clockwise from top left: Plinio Seniore, Villa Borghese, Roma, 2003; Bird, Malibu, Los Angeles, 2000; Extract from diary entry, 2013— ongoing; Caption reading 'thursday 24th', 2003; Birds, Malibu, Los Angeles, 2000

b. Sophy Rickett and Bettina von Zwehl, *Album 31*, 2013. Centrepiece: 36-inch Telescope (built 1951–55), Institute of Astronomy, Cambridge. Clockwise from top left: Cambridge, 2012; Outbox print from *Rain*, 2003 (detail); Outbox print from *Rain*, 2003 (detail); Outbox print from *Rain*, 2003 (detail)

c. Sophy Rickett and Bettina von Zwehl, *Album 31*, 2013. Centrepiece: Still life (ginger on blue), New Inn Broadway, 2012. Clockwise from top left: Clay figurine of woman gazing at sleeping child by Antonia Young, 1998; Dark chocolate Leibniz biscuit fallen to studio floor, 2013; Clay figurine of woman gazing at sleeping child by Antonia Young, 1998; Clay figurine of woman gazing at sleeping child by Antonia Young, 1998

d. Sophy Rickett Bettina and von Zwehl, *Album 31*, 2013. Centrepiece: Barn owl (Tyto alba), Gloucester, 2004. Clockwise from top left: View over South Downs at night from M20 (as seen by BvZ during making of *Untitled Landscape 8*, 1999); Unknown object and reflected light, Glyndebourne, 2007; Oxeye daisies, location unknown, reproduced from the archive of Craig Hutchins, 1970–98; Oxeye daisies, location unknown, reproduced from the archive of Craig Hutchins, 1970–98

e. Sophy Rickett and Bettina von Zwehl, *Album 31*, 2013. Centrepiece: Photo study of Luisa Rovati's hair, Hackney, 1999. Clockwise from top left: Extract from diary entry, 2013—ongoing; Floodlit tree tops, Rome, 2003; Floodlit tree tops, Rome, 2003; Sophy Rickett (accidental self-portrait), Vauxhall Bridge, 1995

f. Sophy Rickett and Bettina von Zwehl, *Album 31*, 2013. Centrepiece: Bunny on mint-green cloth, Whitechapel, 2007. Clockwise from top left: Extract from diary entry, 2013—ongoing; Eye portrait of Mrs Gabriele von Zwehl, née von Wiese und Kaiserswaldau, b. Hamburg, c. 1940, lives and works in Munich, 2012; Eye portrait of psychoanalyst, Hampstead, 2013; Worried child, Belsham Street Studio (top floor), 2005

© Sophy Rickett and Bettina von Zwehl

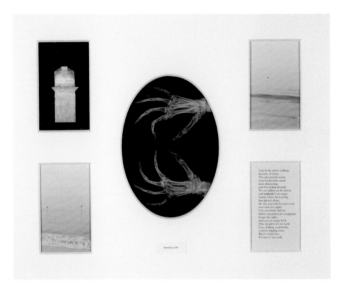

a.

b.

c.

d.

e.

f.

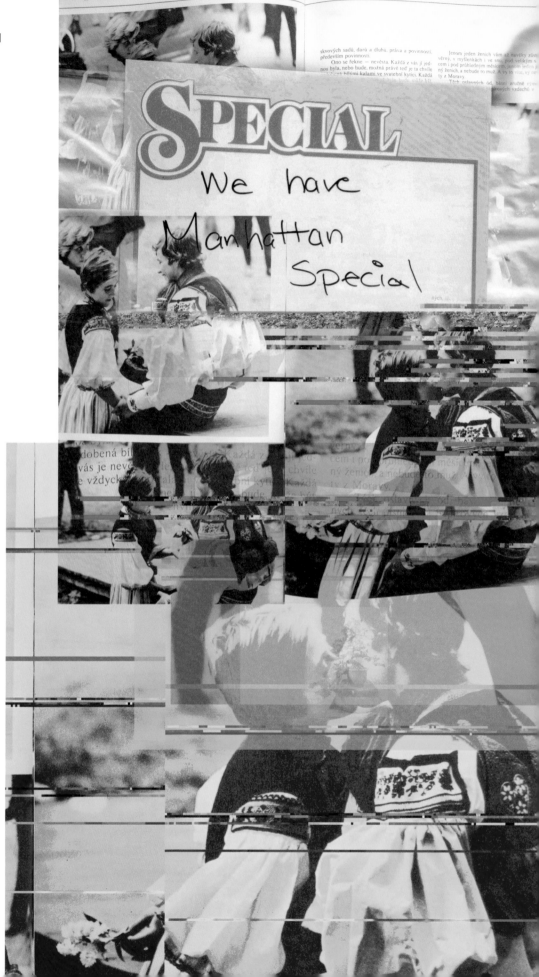

© Michael Rodgers and Nick Scammell

© Michael Rodgers and Nick Scammell

Michael Rodgers and Nick Scammell

I think I can guess what this image is. The red cup suggests that we may be in America. It's one of those American BBQ or New York art world roof-top party cups. The cell-like structure of bubbles, to me, represents the super-size of American soft drinks. The bubbles overfill the cup and require more space to flex their cytoplasmic muscles. America is a culture of *more*: bigger than you and better than you. This could be a Coke float. It could be a milkshake, excited by a straw.

But I don't *know* what this image is. So I can upload it to Google as an image search and find out. It is a bone carving, an owl print stamp, beige in colour, or an opaque glass skull. An algorithm saves the day (again).

The two photographers exchanged pictures from New York, drawing out a narrative of images from their individual experiences of the city. As Vilém Flusser has it, photographs do not represent tangible objects but, rather, experiences. It is on that basis that this collaboration takes place.

Here is a different story.

You don't have to understand every word in a sequence. I'm suspicious of people who seem to understand everything. They jump the gaps; ignore the necessary contradictions and disruptions caused by the words and images we *don't* understand. You have to fake it. This is not fiction. Just a denial of your own ability to remember.

Words reach outwards. They do things to objects through descriptions, adjectives, transitive verbs. If we can call photography a language, then it often seems to be one that speaks to itself. The introspection of the photograph, an object with its own vocabulary. Bring this language to life, transform description into writing through photographing.

Here is a map of remembering. I will have a relationship to this image when I can spot my location on its surface. Digital, interactive maps lift you up to the bird's eye view of the world, full of things you'll never actually see. Like the arrows in the image, you'll be ordered to turn and face a particular way, move in a particular direction. This map is not allowed in Calais. There can be no movement for some.

Spiderman is poised to move, but he is grounded in snow. Like a photograph, the character was exposed to something. A spider senses something that a human can't: humour, for example. Anthropomorphic characters teach us to laugh. How can we predict the future like a photograph? Photographic images don't simply document the past. They imagine the future, too. This is just a photograph of a plastic Spiderman. >

© Michael Rodgers and Nick Scammell

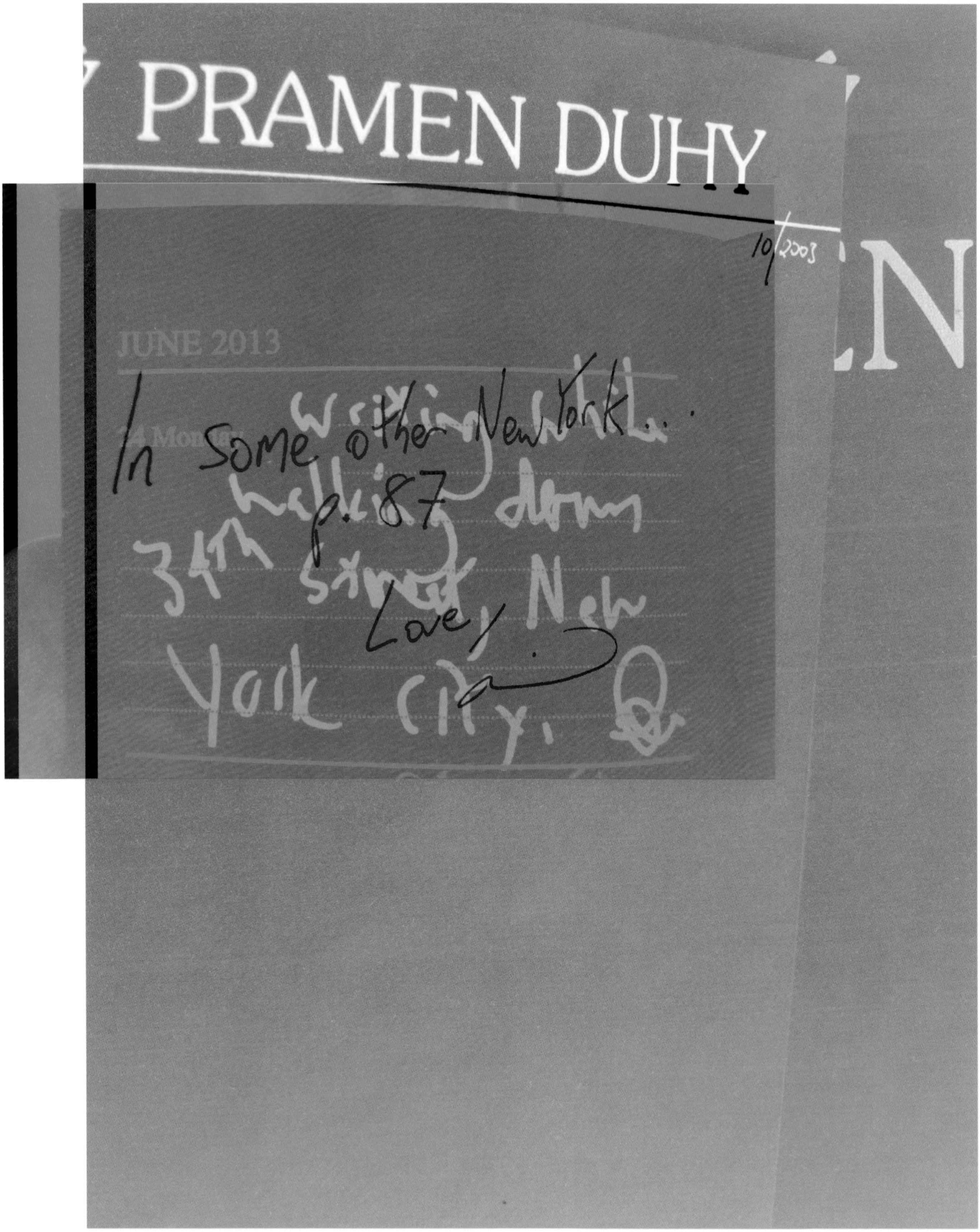
PRAMEN DUHY
10/2003
JUNE 2013
In some other New York...
p. 87
Love,
34th street, New
York City.

Photobattle, Osaka. © Photobattle

Katja Stuke and
Yoshinori Henguchi

Let's return to a face. A face covered in dots. This act prohibits entry but also draws attention to the psychology
of looks. Expression is a strategy. Peering over something. Looking above and beyond an imaginary horizon.
The way you understand your face to carry meaning
is linked to assumptions about the reaction of the person
that meets your gaze, analyses your features, responds
to your profile.

> 'If you have a camera you can make a copy'
> —Daido Moriyama.

Photo Battle is a collaboration that sees two artists
shooting, collaging and responding to a series of encounters—in public space, on the street and in a workshop.
It began in Osaka and continued in Düsseldorf. Taking
its name from the idea of a hip-hop battle, two opponents
are locked in competition and friendship. One of those
photographic flirtations that carries meaning through
a dialogue in images, events and situations.

Images are copied infinitely, so the story goes.

A cut and a corporate typewriter.

Photobattle, Osaka invitation.
© Photobattle

---

1   Sir Benjamin Stone, 'Photographing the deeds' (diary entry), http://
www.search.digitalhandsworth.org.uk (full URL: http://goo.gl/
ydovTo) (17 June 2014).

Photobattle, Osaka. © Photobattle

Photobattle, Düsseldorf.
© Photobattle

Photobattle, Düsseldorf invitation. © Photobattle

Sum of its Parts:
Magnum Collaborations

Nick Galvin

Magnum Photos AGM 2013, London.
© Jonathan Bell

Magnum Photos was founded as a co-operative, and these principles continue to inform the way that Magnum functions. Nick Galvin considers this and other collaborations involved in the global photographic agency, tracing a complex web of creative, commercial and logistical factors.

Martin Parr, *Rusholme, Manchester, England*, 1972.
© Martin Parr/Magnum Photos

In the latest film version of *The Secret Life of Walter Mitty*, the eponymous hero is a negative assets manager at a fictionalised *Life* magazine. Confronted by a vital missing negative, Mitty goes on a quest to track down the photographer, who (in a cameo by Sean Penn) is only seen briefly. Eschewing the technological trappings of modernity, he becomes an emblematic trope of freedom and adventure. He both constructs and reflects a certain nostalgic conception of the photographer as a romantic hero, an outsider above and beyond society. When he is finally tracked down to a distant Afghan mountain, the photographer is cast as Friedrich's wanderer above a sea of fog: a mystic, mythic figure. The photographer becomes a shorthand cipher for the myths we spin around the creative genius: the mad, bad vision of the solitary auteur that underpins many of the narratives of Western art and its atavistic offshoot, the canon of photography.

The film also explores the importance of the 'little guy' as a vital cog in a corporate machine. Walter Mitty is the member of the backroom staff who enables the work of photographers to be published, in contrast to the snide corporate management who are enthusiastically engaged in the shutting of the printed magazine. Though Penn's mythic photographer is set heroically outside of the corporate reality of the publication, he is at the same time placed inside it, via the collaborative links that the film sets up. Explicitly posited outside the grubby world of capital exchange, he remains—by implication, at least—bound to it. The myth of the solitary individual creative genius is punctured. In reality, photographers rely on their collaboration with a complex web of people to make the publication of work possible. Editors, agents, printers and curators all play vital roles, even if, at the instantaneous moment of the shutter click, the photographer has creative control.

The long-departed *Life* magazine has become the stuff of legends, as has one of its most famous luminaries and founding members, Robert Capa. But legends are departures from reality: narratives that conform to our preconceptions of what we want things to be, not as they are. Over its 67-year history, Magnum Photos has accumulated many stories and its fair share of myths. In many of these, the emphasis is on the documentary photographer as the rugged individualist, a solitary observer out in the world, conforming to the romantic ideal. This is only to be expected. The focus on the autonomous creator has been hard-wired into our culture since Romanticism. These narratives tend to overlook the fact that Magnum is not just a collection of photographers but also a functioning agency that operates in a nexus of political, economic, social and technological relations. The photographers are not creating works of art in some kind of pure Edenic state but commodities for commercial exchange. They respond to the editorial constraints rooted in commercial concerns. The interplay of collaboration between photographer, staff and client is writ large. >

Most people are aware that photographers have to work to earn a living. Magnum photographers are no exception. As such, they know that collaboration is a necessary aspect of photographic production and distribution. At a recent launch for volume III of his *The Photobook: A History*, Martin Parr recognised the importance of the graphic designer in the creation of photographic monographs. Indeed, the insightful and amusing 2010 documentary *How to Make a Book with Steidl*, featured Parr alongside other luminaries, including Jeff Wall, Robert Frank and Joel Sternfeld, as they received intricate and hands-on production guidance from the publisher Gerhard Steidl. This is not a recent phenomenon. Henri Cartier-Bresson himself had notable associations with the publisher and editor Robert Delpire, and his main printer, Pierre Gassman. Other photographers have had similar long-term collaborations, such as Rene Burri and Hans-Michael Koetzle, who have worked on various projects since the publication of Burri's retrospective.

In 1947, at the birth of Magnum, Robert Capa collaborated with John Steinbeck on the acclaimed *Russian Journal*, written as a travelogue for the *New York Tribune* just as the temperature began to drop in the Cold War. Yet, in the age of online dispersal and the appropriation of documentary as exhibited art, Capa's Russian images of collective farm workers have become entirely divorced from Steinbeck's text, just as Walker Evans's seminal work on dustbowl sharecroppers is rarely seen with James Agee's text in *Now Let Us Praise Famous Men*. This divorcing of photographic content from its original context is symptomatic of post-modernity. Myths accumulate in the gaps that result. The idea of the lone photographer as solitary hero takes hold, obscuring parts of this collaborative past.

Collaborative photographic partnerships are becoming increasingly common. The Gao Brothers, Pierre et Gilles, and Broomberg and Chanarin are partnerships that need little introduction. Such associations have existed for Magnum photographers too. Trent Parke worked with his wife, Narelle Autio, on the book *A Seventh Wave*, offering an oblique underwater look at Australian beach culture. Alex Webb has a long collaboration with his wife, photographer and poet Rebecca Norris. According to the accepted legend, even 'Robert Capa' was originally a concept created out of the relationship between Andre Freidmann and Gerda Taro, in a ploy to help the impoverished Freedman sell his work. With a conjured *nom de plume*, Capa was invented to be a successful and famous American photographer. They would work together in the Spanish Civil War. Following Taro's untimely death in 1937, her own images of the war became somewhat intertwined with Capa's more famous work. It was only after the discovery of the Mexican Suitcase in 2007, containing original negatives, that Taro's work could be unpicked from the whole and her own authorial identity made fully visible again. >

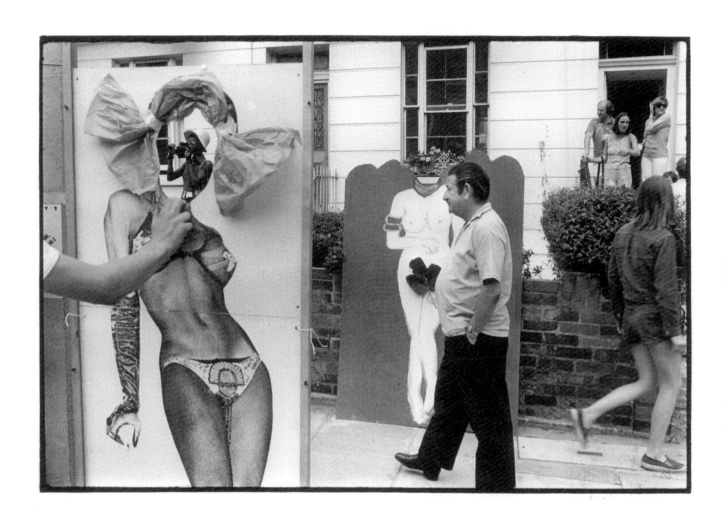

Chris Steele-Perkins, *Camden Street Festival, London*, 1975.
© Chris Steele-Perkins/Magnum Photos

Rene Burri, *Bomb Craters Near the Cambodia Border,*
South Vietnam, 1973. © Rene Burri/Magnum Photos

Aspects of Magnum's institutional practices unwittingly help to obscure these photographic partnerships. A photographer must join the co-operative as an individual. Technological systems of image management—the alphanumeric cataloguing system and the database architecture—encode and attribute work on an individual basis. This is by no means limited to Magnum: Western cultural notions of copyright, property and ownership predicated on the individual form a deep armature to which universal technical and financial systems comply.

Magnum was founded on the principles of giving photographers authorial control. But, as a co-operative, ideas of collaboration are also built into the very foundations of the agency. Unlike with the usual proprietorial agency, the photographers are not separate individuals working for a company, they are an integral part. Every year they gather at the AGM, a time when they can review the business, set policies for its governance and share new work. Most importantly, they vote to choose new members. Like the Vatican papal elections, this collaborative process is highly secret, a fact that helps generate its own further mythology.

Collaboration becomes more visible when Magnum photographers work together for a common aim. Many recent projects have involved photographers coming together for group exhibitions and book projects, often with external partners. Instigated in Magnum's New York office in 2007, the *Access to Life* collaboration between The Global Fund and Magnum resulted in eight photographers documenting the impact of AIDS and HIV on 30 people in nine countries throughout the world. After being exhibited at the Corcoran Gallery of Art in the US, under the aegis of curator Bill Horrigan, it became an acclaimed touring show with an accompanying online presence and a book published by the Aperture Foundation. The online credits reveal a complex web of curators, editors, designers and staff as well as patrons who were instrumental in bringing the exhibition, website and book together. This collaborative model has become more prevalent in Magnum since digitisation altered traditional commissioning and licencing income from magazines and newspapers.

Euro Visions, The New Europeans provides a similar European example from the same period. Fifty years since Cartier-Bresson's acclaimed *Europeans* and the Treaty of Rome, *Euro Visions* was conceived as a group project with the Centre Pompidou. Each Magnum photographer provided a personal vision in one of the 12 new member countries in the EU. Curated by the then Magnum Paris director Diane Dufour and Quentin Bajac, the curator at the Musée National d'Art Moderne, the show first appeared at the Centre Pompidou in Paris in 2005, before traveling to Milan, Budapest and Warsaw. The tour ended in Brussels in time for the 50th anniversary of the Treaty of Rome celebrations in 2007.

In these projects, the photographers pursued individual and personal visions. But, in collaborating and co-operating with curators, this creative autonomy was shaped by the external curatorial process. Just as the auteur theory of cinema breaks down when the complex interrelations of the production team are considered, the idea of the photographer as a fully autonomous and independent author comes under similar strain. The digital paradigm has increasingly allowed photographers to assert their singular voice via websites and self-publishing (indeed, it has become necessary for them to assert a personal expressiveness in order to counter the plurality and ubiquity of the digital image). But, at the same time, this individuality is undercut by the realities of production and the collaborative nature of commerce. This is no bad thing: the overall body of work by the individual authors of Magnum has been enriched by its various collaborations and co-operations over the years. Underlying all of this remains the important fact that Magnum itself is a collaboration; a coming together of like-minded creative photographers for a common aim.

Though mythic photographers may still, on occasion, stand on lonely mountains above the world, the reality of Magnum is that the photographers are part of a wider collaborative network.

The images reproduced alongside this article form part of *One Archive, Three Views*, a new BPB commission. Magnum, De La Warr Pavilion and Photoworks invited visual anthropologist Elizabeth Edwards, photographer Hannah Starkey and multi-media artist Uriel Orlow to use the Magnum archives, comprising over 68,000 prints, as the basis for new curated works. Their responses reflect on the social, cultural and political pressures that have shaped the archive and the history of Magnum.

Round Table:

Community Photography,

Now and Then

BEN BURBRIDGE
ANTHONY LUVERA
MATT DAW
ANDREW DEWDNEY
NONI STACEY
EUGENIE DOLBERG

Our round-table discussion explores the histories of community photography in Britain, questions what terms such as 'participation' really mean, and considers the implications of the current art world interest in collaborative practices.

BB: Recent years have witnessed an increased interest in what could be described in terms of 'community photography'—collaborative or participatory photo practices in which traditional relationships between makers, subjects and audiences become complicated in one way or another. Much of this interest has come from within the art world. I am thinking about projects by people like Susan Meiselas, Monica Haller, Jim Goldberg, and, of course, by Eugenie and Anthony here with us. So, I wanted to start off by thinking about the potential histories with which we can provide this kind of work.

AL: I think it involves a convergence of a number of different histories—there isn't just one. There are some strong voices within the critiques of documentary photography from the 1980s, for example. People such as Martha Rosler, Abigail Solomon-Godeau and Allan Sekula called for a more open view of the production of the documentary-making process. They felt that relations between the subject, photographer and medium should be cracked open somehow.

NS: But also earlier than that, the radical photo magazine *Camerawork* was examining all of those boundaries between the producers and distributors of photographs, and between picture editors, journalists and photographers. Those practitioners were looking back, again, to groups working in the 1930s who had also examined those boundaries.

AL: Another dialogue comes out of conceptual art practices that emerged in the late 1960s and 1970s. Particularly those that centred on self-reflexive investigations through performance or participation, such as work by Douglas Huebler, Wendy Ewald, Suzanne Lacy, Mierle Laderman Ukeles, Stephen Willats, John Latham and the Artist Placement Group.

AD: There is little map of histories emerging here …

AL: I see it as a map of circles converging on each other …

AD: Which reflects the fact that photography was being taken up and used in a number of different institutional contexts. We should also think about urban politics and community arts. This

Cover of *Camerawork*, 'Photography in the Community', 1979

didn't necessarily involve photography but did involve situations in which artists were working with young people. Adventure playgrounds were important too. In my own experience of meeting young people, youth clubs and informal educational situations were important places where photography was promoted as a hobby or as an accessible kind of practice. It was seen as something that was both enjoyable and also allowed people to make images of their own lives and situations.

NS: Community photography was directly engaged with politics too. It was linked to community activism, history from below, a challenge to the canon and the academy.

AD: So we can think about community politics in the form of things like print workshops, legal aid and community workshops in places like Paddington. In these contexts, photography often became this very useful, mobilising means to campaign

about something, housing for instance. On the other hand, documentary photographers like Robert McCormack wanted to come in and connect with these kinds of politics: showing conditions, showing how people live. So I think there is convergence of all those different interests, rooted in the politics of Britain in the 1970s and 1980s. The election of Margaret Thatcher is vitally important to this history: the sense that the post-war gains of social democracy were on the line due to hospital closures, the introduction of the national curriculum and so on.

Photojournalists, documentarians, artists, activists and community artists all saw photography as a means. In *Camerawork* and, later, *Ten.8*, photography was used to show another kind of life that was absent from mainstream media. At that time, Rupert Murdoch owned and promoted a certain view of the world, which many of these groups opposed. Northern Ireland is a very good example of this. People went there, took different pictures and printed them in their own magazines because, without that, people would not see that view due to the agendas of the mainstream right-wing press.

AL: I think that was one of the impetuses that drove the collective of photographers that formed Belfast Exposed. They were dissatisfied with the way in which photojournalists and documentarians were coming to Belfast to represent the main events of the Troubles. They wanted to speak directly to the people of Belfast, in both the Protestant and Catholic areas of the city, to say 'What does the real Belfast look like to you?', and then they began touring these exhibitions and hosting workshops.

I sometimes feel disconnected from the landscape we are talking about because the histories of community photography haven't been very clearly written. Su Braden's *Committing Photography*, from 1983, is perhaps one of the only publications that charts the early history of community photography in the UK. It's very difficult to speak about a clean history for the collaborative photography practices of today.

NS: Both you and Eugenie describe yourselves as artists, and that signals an important shift. In the 1970s there was no concern about calling yourself an artist if you were involved in efforts to challenge photojournalism or documentary,

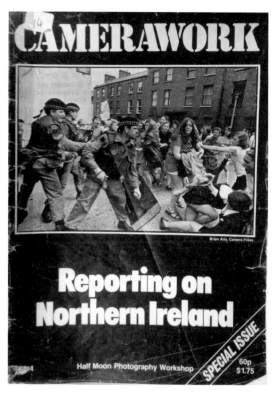

Cover of *Camerawork*, 'Reporting on Northern Ireland', 1979

or just working in a darkroom. For *Camerawork* what mattered was not 'Is it art?' but 'Who is it for?' Many of the current practices are very much engaged with aesthetic theory and those sorts of areas.

AL: From my point of view, I am more interested in thinking about 'Who is the audience?' rather than 'Where is the art?', and this is one of the reasons I am often keen to use the public domain to present my work. I try to speak to multiple audiences, which isn't to say I am adverse to working in a gallery. I do have a gallery practice.

MD: Thinking about this history, it seems as if we could have reached the current moment even if there hadn't been any participatory photo practice until the 1990s. It seems to get reinvented at every stage, more so than any other art practice I've encountered.

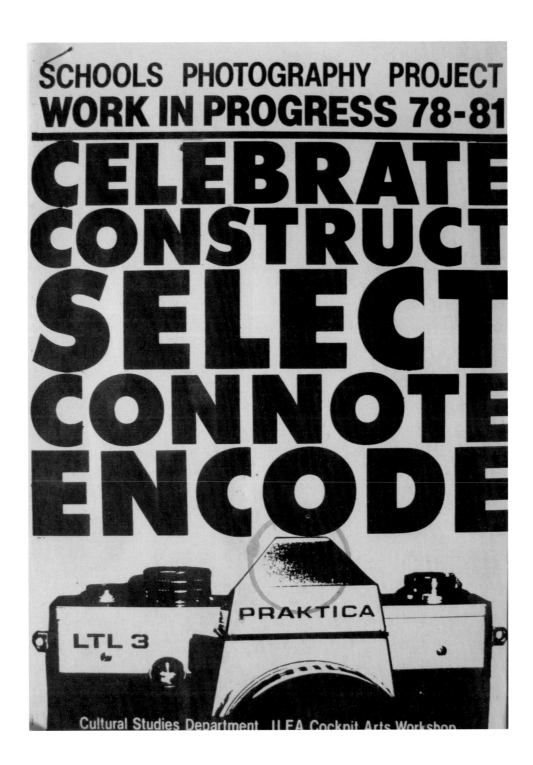

'Schools Photography Project', publication, 1978–81

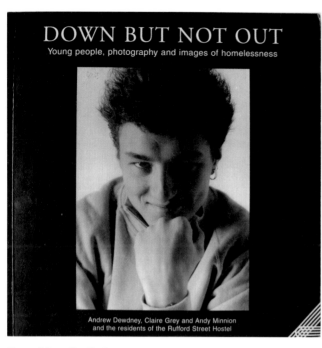

Cover of *Down But Not Out*, 1994

AL: It's one of the interesting things that Jo Spence and Terry Dennett spoke about in the mid-1970s: there needs to be a mapping, a telling of the history of community photography practices, otherwise practitioners will go on reinventing the wheel.

MD: Do you think that absence reflects the status of community photography? It always feels marginal to something else.

AD: It has never been invisible, but it's been so separate from the mainstream. Everything seems like a little satellite project that comments on something very specific. No-one is linking up practices with each other. They only recognise what that specific project is commenting on in the mainstream media.

NS: I don't know. All of the 1970s projects I've been looking at were interrelated. All across London, these people knew what each other were doing, in terms of the debates and the practices.

The photographers were either working at or contributing to *Camerawork*, they weren't working in isolation.

AD: Of course the darkroom was very important—you had community darkrooms in an analogue world, and that provided a very productive meeting place.

ED: It's interesting to listen to this discussion, because I came to this kind of work from a completely different position. I was working as a photojournalist, and I reacted to the media and the frustrations I experienced. The largest body of work that I made in Iraq was a reaction to the logistical limitations being imposed on photojournalism in 2006. Journalists were targets, and so were the people who they were in contact with. In that sense, the stories coming out of Iraq were purely from government or military sources. I could see there was another sort of way to make those stories, and that was really how I came into it, not from a historical point of view. So it's really interesting listening to you talk, but I don't really feel like I can engage.

NS: I used to work in newsrooms, so I've worked in that world. Now you've got Reuters, you've got AP—you've got these extraordinary monolithic news organisations. It's very difficult to circumvent them.

ED: That's what I found. I became a photographer because I believe in the power of stories. And I am political—that was really my motivation for becoming a photographer. Then, when I worked within the kind of environment you're describing, I found that that wasn't the best way for these stories to come out.

I was meeting people and hearing stories in the first person, and it was so much more powerful. Actually, I felt that the people with whom I was working, who were my 'passive subjects' in a way, were brilliant and articulate and very, very capable of representing themselves. I felt that people just weren't interested in those voices and were very dismissive. It has been a very interesting journey for me.

The Iraq project was put into the 'participatory photography' bracket, and since then I have struggled with that label. I wonder if, had I possessed more knowledge of the historical or the academic context and really understood what that term actually meant, I would have accepted it or, instead, insisted on the project as a political feminist action made by a group of women that should not be dismissed as a fluffy project working with sweet little women in Iraq. And, to be honest, that is how I found a lot of the mainstream has looked at the work. To me, it was a really radical, brave, action taken by a group of women who collaborated together at great personal risk, showing great commitment, with nothing in it for them other than to say, 'We will not be written out of history.'

BB: It's an important point, which raises some difficult questions about the type of history we began to describe earlier. Is it appropriate for practices to be defined as fundamentally and primarily participatory or collaborative? Does that risk ghettoising the work? On the one hand, it seems important to be able to access that history; on the other hand, I can see how that can raise problems.

Cover of *Racism, Representation and Photography*, 1994

AD: One of the problems is the question of 'whose history?', and that was what was being dealt with in that particular period of the 1970s. I think there is a continuity between what Eugenie has said and what Jo Spence might have said in terms of the Hackney Flashers. Remember there were probably only a dozen degree courses in photography in the country at the time. If you were political you didn't want to be in the mainstream, but you saw that the mainstream controlled the big story, and you were looking for ways of intervening in or opposing it. So, I think there is a massive, interesting continuity, which is a reinvention—it's a personal reinvention, as well as a kind of social and political reinvention.

BB: In narrating this history, you have focused on a period in the 1970s and early 1980s as a kind of 'golden age'. This seems to position the current work as a recent re-emergence. What happened in between? Did this kind of work just disappear?

AL: I'm not sure there was a disappearance altogether. Maybe it was re-routed. It seems to me that there is also a discussion to be had around the learning and participation agendas of museums and other state-funded audience development activities. The majority of what we might call community photography now takes place there and lacks the sort of dialectical voice that you've spoken about. It lacks the kind of impetus for making work that Eugenie described, which was also important for my work with homeless people in London. I didn't grow up with community photography. I had never been to a community art group or to an adventure playground. My interests grew out of thinking about representation and being asked to make photographs of homeless people, and reacting to that.

AD: During the 1990s we witnessed a major repositioning of photography. There was a massive expansion of photography in higher education as it became something that middle-class parents were happy for their kids to do, sometimes just as much as had they done law or medicine. Photography also got repositioned in contemporary art, and that is a very important factor here. I am not sure how that affects

Antoinette lives in Mosul and made her story in 2007. Her black and white photographs are motherhood with all the love and silent struggle it entails.

     She is Christian. In July 2014, ISIS captured Mosul and ordered all Christians to convert, pay impossible taxes or face execution. Photographs and videos of beheaded Christians littered the internet.

'I am torn. My life and that of my kids is in Mosul—our house, our memories, everything that we know and that means anything to us. But, am I not being unfair to them if I choose to stay? And if I left, where would I go? What kind of future can I possibly offer them? I feel exhausted, drained, but all that disappears the minute I hear my children giggling, or calling "Mum". I feel then that everything is worth it.'

Um Mohammad was from Basra. She watched her own identity being stripped from her as her city was destroyed and taken over by religious parties and militias. Her photographs are loving portraits of Basra, resonating loss and time past.

'Everything in my city has been looted, stolen and burned. The British army has done nothing about it. They just laughed and called the thieves and destroyers the Ali Babas of Basra. We visited this ruined piece of land many times when it used to be an amusement park. After the occupation, the rides were all stolen, and even the bricks. And, for some inexplicable reason, the palm trees were burned down.'

All images © Um Mohammad/Index on Censorship/ Open Shutters

Um Mohammad lived in an area heavily affected by depleted uranium. She died of cancer on 25 January 2009

Eugenie Dolberg, from *Open Shutters Iraq*, 2010

the dialectic you are describing. Perhaps these art spaces are themselves new spaces for politics. That was definitely not true in the 1970s. The mainstream arts, the national institutions, were profoundly uninterested in photography. At that time, for art, it was business as usual. It was a bourgeois pursuit. It was only in the very margins of museum learning and outreach programmes that any other sort of discourse or audience was being considered. So, I wonder what are the tensions for current practitioners in terms of this repositioning of photography within contemporary art practice? Does it allow you to hold onto the kind of things that you said are political in your work?

AL: For me, it's about trying to find opportunities for the work to be seen in different types of context, not only within the context of photography publications or the art world but also within discussions that are based in visual anthropology, sociology, housing—discussions that take place that are directly related to the work.

ED: It has a lot to do with audience and accessibility, but also legitimacy. It provides a kind of public recognition for the work.

AL: I have struggled with the term 'community photography'. I remember when I was working in Belfast and was reaching the point of presenting the work, I was having conversations—really critical, thorough conversations—with the curator around things like press releases, interpretation texts and that sort of stuff. I really wanted to be true to the fact that my interests were about exploring the perspectives of the people I was looking at and looking with, as opposed to being a kind of 'community photographer'.

    The whole notion of community is thorny. When making *Not Going Shopping* with a group of queer people in Brighton, the idea of a queer community was picked at throughout our discussions. It felt much more appropriate, and accurate, to speak of communities—plural —of lesbian, gay, bisexual and trans* people, rather than the one LGBT* community.

ED: To be honest, I am struggling with all of that at the moment. I really struggle with the word

'community' for a start. I also struggle with the term 'participatory photography' because it is such a broad term and there is so much bad practice. I am going to talk frankly: there is so much bad practice and so many do-good, damaging, crappy, boring projects. I feel like I can't really speak in this conversation because we are using terms that I don't think I understand or can define.

AD: How would you use 'community' in relationship to your work?

ED: If we are talking about the Iraq project, people told me that this wasn't a community and I couldn't make the work because everyone was going to kill each other. It was the height of the sectarian violence and I was bringing together Ba'athists, people's families who had been killed by Ba'athists, Shias, Sunnis, Christians, and I was adamant that I wasn't going to start labelling people or start splitting them up according to those labels and constructed communities.

    In a way that was part of my personal action and, again, it's a sort of feminist action, in that we were looking at a particular layer of conflict, a domestic layer that is largely ignored and dismissed. The methodology that we used was a reaction to the need to work with these particular stories.

AD: But wasn't there something those women shared, if we are trying to unpick this idea of what constitutes community?

ED: Absolutely. The common thing for us as a group of women was that we felt that women's experiences should no longer be written out of history. But a lot of people are still dismissive of the work, and I wonder whether that's because it has been situated in the context of participatory photography. When I would approach a museum and say I have a participatory photography project I felt that, quite often, people were dismissive because of the terminology and what they understood it to mean.

MD: I have similar frustrations at PhotoVoice. Many of our projects involve incredibly important stories. They often present unheard and very valid viewpoints on an issue that the media *is*

Lujane lives in Baghdad. She went to work
but was distraught at how empty her city had
become. Determined to show what had become
of her once bustling city, she took an eerie
series of empty cityscapes.

'Al Umara' was the best restaurant and pa-
tisserie in Baghdad. It's in the Karrada area,
which was relatively safe at the start of the
occupation. My father used to love to buy
us baklava from there. Now, life has stopped
in Karrada because of all the bombings. Inno-
cent people are slaughtered in the Islamic way,
of course—"Halal butchery"!'

All images ©Lujane/Index on Censorship/
Open Shutters

talking about. But the media will usually see it as a story about a participatory photography project—that's what they want to feature. Our original mission statement, written eight years ago, included something about trying to get underrepresented voices into the media. But we've realised that isn't something we can really commit to doing because we are completely in sway to mechanisms that we have no control over. What we can do is designate a specific agenda, a specific intended outcome from a specific project. If we just thought of participatory photography as a means in and of itself, which would bring benefits regardless, then we would have some serious issues.

NS: There was much debate about the term 'community' earlier on. It wasn't happily received in the 1970s and early 1980s.

AD: It was fought over by feminists and Marxists.

ED: In post-conflict Belfast there's some amazing examples. It feels as though there's been so much community funding that it has helped to actually structure the communities there. It's a business. There has been so much money pumped into community work and community projects that some of these things have been constructed as a consequence.

BB: So there is an interesting discussion to be had around the criteria used to evaluate these types of project, much of which seems to be driven by economics. Our precise understanding of these kinds of practice shifts according to the particular funding base on which they draw. A project funded by an NGO suggests a very different agenda to one that relies on Arts Council money.

AD: And funding is tied up with politics. To return to our previous example, *Camerawork*'s focus on Northern Ireland was very clearly framed: 'The British state is prosecuting a war against the Irish people, we are behind the Troops Out movement, we will mobilise our representations to fit this kind of opposition to the British state.' Wind forward to now, and it seems incredibly difficult to make that kind of statement. There are still tiny little splinter groups on the Left and sects who would say noth-

Documentation of the making of *Assisted Self-Portrait of Joe Murray*, from *Residency*, 2006–08 by Anthony Luvera. © Joe Murray/Anthony Luvera

ing's changed but, of course, everything has changed, and that's the problem for all of us sitting in this room. We have to try to get through the complexities of this kind of politics in order to feel that what we are doing is authentic, that it does actually identify what is progressive as opposed to what has been hijacked for some other agenda. The whole idea of community was hijacked and made passive by New Labour. Community became a passive term rather than a critical and oppositional one.

ED: Participation and communities can so often be taken as an equal good, and I think that should be questioned. Within the context of my current research, I am starting to question whether participation does necessarily equal good. At which point is participation good and at which point is it actually redundant and unhelpful?

NS: To really think about that we would have to hear from voices outside of this room, from those who contribute to these projects. What's their involvement in saying how it was and how it worked for them?

AL: Participation always takes place within the terms of an invitation, and someone either buys into wanting to take part or doesn't.

MD: If we are talking about participation, we should also talk about control. When talking about participation photography, some people simply mean they're not the one holding the camera. But they are controlling the agenda. They're controlling everything, but they're billing it as a participatory project and they are not defining what that means. Or, if they do, they define it in the highest possible terms, saying this is an 'empowering project' because these people are the ones taking the pictures. That relies on a general naivety about the forms of participation that are actually possible in a particular context.

 PhotoVoice started in a very ideological way, and we became more realistic about what forms of participation are—in actuality—socially beneficial. We now think it is absolutely imperative that you are communicating to the community that you are working in in order for it to understand the real level of participation. If you're inviting the community to contribute to a project that is focused on a specific issue, it should know that from the start, so that is what they are choosing to participate in.

BB: So, you hope the work will be 'socially beneficial'?

MD: Yes. That's PhotoVoice's term because we're not involved with art practice.

BB: What exactly does it mean in this context?

MD: It requires us to define aspects of social change that we want to work towards and the extent to which we feel a project will contribute to that. We define that for each project but, whatever the definition, we are trying to give an active role to people who would not otherwise be involved in that process of social change.

BB: So, in determining the value of a PhotoVoice project, the main criterion you would use is the 'social change' achieved? Anthony and Eugenie, your work engages much more explicitly with the discourses of fine art, as well as documentary and photojournalism. So, what criteria would you use?

Assisted Self-Portrait of Joe Murray, from *Residency*, 2006–08
by Anthony Luvera. © Joe Murray/Anthony Luvera

Polaroid from the making of *Assisted Self-Portrait of Joe Murray*,
from *Residency*, 2006–08 by Anthony Luvera.
© Joe Murray/Anthony Luvera

Photograph by Maggie Irvine from *Residency*, 2006–08
by Anthony Luvera. © Anthony Luvera

AL: I think this whole idea of values, benefits and outcomes is totally problematic. I often describe my work as being socially engaged, and I am interested in looking at the social realities of the people with whom I work. Through this I hope to shake up or challenge preconceptions about the experiences of those individuals, but I am not in the business of saying that my work improves people's self-confidence or self-esteem or that it creates social change.

MD: I would define individual change as separate from social change. In our projects, the process is more likely to contribute to individual change, and the project as a whole is going to be about social change.

BB: Can you give us a specific example?

MD: When we get called to work in a certain context we consider two sides of the project. One would be the process, which of course encapsulates all sorts of practical things like risks: are we going to bring together a group of people who are going to put themselves at risk or kill each other or whatever? We also think about the actual benefits or potential benefits of the process for those people. On the other side, we think about the potential result of these voices being heard because, in the end, photography is a form of communication, and what we are doing is bridging a gap by creating some kind of communication.

AL: So, who's defining those ambitions and intentions? Is that through the sort of funding stream criteria you need to match up to?

MD: It varies. We develop some projects ourselves where we feel they possess a particular value. For example, in our current Shutter Release programme we are mainly working around the justice system, focusing on people who are trying to rehabilitate or bring about change in their life. This project is entirely process-driven, so, although there are some public outputs, they are simply what those involved choose to release. Some bits get shown, but most of the work doesn't get released.

BB: So, the project aims to achieve a kind of personal, therapeutic benefit?

MD: It's not phototherapy, but it should certainly be seen in a therapeutic context. We bring in a psychotherapist alongside the workshop process to enable that. So, we responded to a perceived social need and tried to get funding for it. With another current project, the Voice of Freedom, we are working with women who have been trafficked in order to address advocacy issues. There are a lot of potential benefits for the women involved in the process, but that's not actually why we are running the project. From a funder's point of view, our goal is to contribute their voices to advocacy messaging. Most of the money is from private funders so, while they don't actually require very much, they are not going to be too impressed if we say we need £20,000 to benefit six or ten people.

NS: A lot of these projects address a generic human rights agenda. The discussion has moved away from the local and the political concerns that informed previous practices. In a way, it's become more global.

AD: It is centred on the individual. One of the other elusive notions about community is that it was actually about the bonds between people, about the life and the world they shared. It was based in place more than anything else, but also in work and tradition. More recently, the sense of the social democratic has moved to the individual and human rights because everybody can get that. We don't understand what class we belong to, we are very confused with ideas about gender, we are pretty uncertain about community. So, what can we all get? This idea that 'we are all individuals and we should all be equal'. It's a politics that can be progressive in terms of social change, but it's also a politics of commodity, of lifestyle and charity. It's another minefield.

NS: I think that's why this whole agenda of participatory photography has been very much adopted by NGOs. It fits neatly into their remit. It is understandable and acceptable.

ED: Which may be one reason why it gets dismissed by the art world. And there is a huge difference between the art world and the NGO world. The intentions informing the use of participatory photography by NGOs is so different

from the use of elements of participatory photography in work like Anthony's or mine. For us to be labelled in the same way, or situated under the same umbrella, is quite frustrating. That's what I was trying to say earlier—in part it is an issue with language. We get grouped together under these huge words that actually are so broad that they have no meaning.

MD: They will always rely on the specific context in which they are being used. We used to do some projects focused in the art field and some that were directed more at development.

ED: I very much agree with what Anthony said about where he situates his work. I find the whole language around power and these kinds of projects really dangerous, actually. You don't give power, you take it, so the idea of empowering somebody is, to me, really quite scary. In developing a potential project in Belfast, I am currently spending a six-month period trying to meet with the people I might work with so that we at least have some feeling that

we are involved in a collaborative process, that this is an action we are taking together. There is so much hierarchical language around this work, and I find myself very uncomfortable with the language being used. Even the word 'project' implies that something needs changing, and I don't necessarily think that's what I am interested in.

AL: It also imposes a time limit on things when, in fact, these things should be open ended.

MD: I find it really dangerous not to define things in terms of a project because if it is so open ended you can never say whether or not it was worth doing.

NS: But I wish some of the work was more open ended. We are losing that sort of engagement with local communities. PhotoVoice is doing a lot of projects abroad, and I think it's a shame that more things aren't being done in cities. In the 1970s there was a re-imagining of the cities—there were squats, there was dereliction, there was appalling housing, and photographers responded to that.

AD: I think there is a different kind of time frame involved in all of this now. Years ago, people might live somewhere for a long time. They would be part of a world or a community as a photographer. That's clear in Judy Harrison's recent book. She was absolutely amazed to be given an honour by the Sikh community that she has worked with for over 20 years. That book was 20 years in the making. And it feels like it comes from a different world to a project like Voices of Freedom. Both are voices of freedom in the broad sense, but one is rooted in speed and global relationships, which is the complete opposite to Judy's kind of project.

AL: The idea of time and temporality in these sorts of practices is incredibly interesting, and there seems to be a perceived idea that short-termism is bad and long-termism is good. But I'm not sure that is necessarily the case. We need to think instead about the terms, the

intentions and the ambitions of the practitioner along with the dialogues and relationships they develop. Underpinning all of this are relationships with people. It's very human. The process involved in work like Eugenie's is rooted in human relationships.

NS: But those take time to develop, and they change over time.

AL: The internet has become a fantastic way for me to develop and maintain relationships with participants and also to think about what this idea of community involves for the people I work with. I feel very uneasy about the word 'community' as we have already discussed, and I always try to use the term 'groups of people' or the plural, 'communities'. But whether or not I am still in contact with people shouldn't be used as a means by which a value judgement should be made about my work.

MD: One of the things that I like about defining things as projects as opposed to part of the

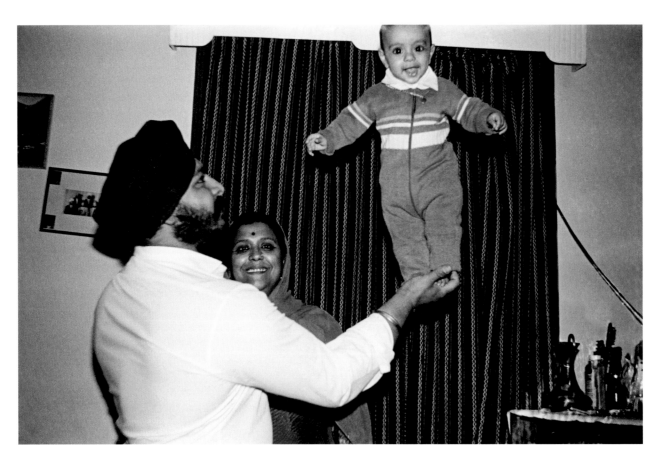

practice of an artist or facilitator is that it focuses attention on the voices of the people who are actually taking the photographs.

AL: As well as the voice of your organisation, of course. PhotoVoice always needs to think about its marketing agenda within the production of a project.

MD: I'm not suggesting we are invisible.

AL: Of course not, but I think the visibility of the organisation needs to be taken into consideration.

MD: We often start off a process, and other organisations continue it. I would situate a lot of what we do in the international development field. To cite another example, I am going on a second trip to Zimbabwe next month to follow up on a project for which representatives from different villages have been provided with cameras and trained in photography. We have set up a local system whereby they meet and have opportunities to download and view each other's photos and discuss them. It is facilitated by a few local organisations, and we are just dipping back into that process to evaluate what has happened since, and then it will carry on in perpetuity.

We are not going to curate any artistic output from this, and we are not going to make any social conclusions. It's a process, and that will inform development practices out there. But, for me, those people are now photographers, community photographers if you like, and there is a kind of legacy, which is independent of the intentions of the project. Those people have developed a network, they've forged connections, they know where to get prints made, they know various ways to create a livelihood from it.

AD: It's a reverse engineering of colonialism. There is a version of that in the art world, a belief in somehow turning back the whole global moment of capitalism through a series of moves. Of course, the project may have meaning and significance for local people in Zimbabwe, but it's of an order that wasn't mapped within the intentions of the project. I don't know how reflexive the organisation is about what it is doing. This is not a criticism, it's a question about a situation in which human rights politics have been projected onto everybody. It is very different to working on some crap estate around the corner. But, of course, you can do both, and both are sites of engagement or participation.

MD: Well, because we do both we have shied away from making a broad description of what our work contributes on the world-stage—it would be too difficult. We have to tie the agenda of each project to the story of that project. We describe ourselves as experts in participatory photography as a mechanism. There isn't anything else that actually ties all of our work together.

ED: I am working with a friend of mine at the moment, trying to write my own manifesto that separates me from all of this. There's so much that I don't identify with there. I'm not saying it's wrong, but I don't identify with it. We all come to this table with different relationships to this kind of work, different interests, different points of connection with it. It really is a minefield. I sometimes find myself having a sort of negative physical reaction to words like 'participatory photography', because there's so much participatory photography practice that I don't identify with. When I break it down and try to look at the linguistics, it becomes very complicated. What's the difference between collaboration and participation, for example? Even the title of 'artist' is new to me, because I am a photographer who doesn't really take photographs any more. So, I'm not really a photographer, I am really trying to redefine myself.

BB: We have discussed a variety of ways in which this kind of work can potentially be judged, in terms of the quality of social relationships involved, an ability to disrupt power structures …

NS: We have also talked about engagement in the local, national, global …

BB: Absolutely, but we haven't spoken about aesthetics, about the way these photographs actually look. Do those issues matter here?

AL: The aesthetics or appearance of my work comes about through the particular kind of methodologies and processes by which I use equipment with participants. It is also directly informed by the various discussion-based activities undertaken to shape the work and make decisions about what can and can't be used, and how and where it can be used. As an author, I am always looking around for opportunities for the work to be seen in what I think are the right contexts for it. So, I am quite happy to call myself the author of the projects I undertake, because I am the one who is out there trying to show them to other people. But, within this, I think it is important to be aware of issues to do with intention and ambition, context and reception, and to think reflectively about my place within all of these.

To look at work created through participation and to judge it based purely on the aesthetic of the material presented—the styles, the sort of medium, all of that stuff—that is inconsequential. It is insufficient. We are talking about relationships that take place over time through very particular processes, methodologies and interactions. That's where the work takes place. For me, this process is as much the 'art' as the objects that are created or displayed to the public. The work wouldn't exist had the process not unfolded in the way it did.

BB: Is 'inconsequential' overstating the case? Looking at any number of recent publications, it is clear a lot of thought has gone into what both the photographs and the books look like. They look really good.

AD: There is something very paradoxical about this. There is a book by a group of artists in New York called *Undoing Property*, and it is a most beautiful book, it's a wonderful piece of property, and that irony is not lost on the artists either. For me, it's not that these issues are inconsequential—I think the paradox itself is the important thing.

MD: It's not like you're ever really going to step back and say that these photographs are more attractive, more powerful, more memorable than those ones over there. I'm just trying to define what make a participatory photography account different from someone going into a similar situation as a professional photographer. When you come to appreciate who is holding the camera, then things change. It is not just how beautiful the photograph is and whether

it uses the rule of thirds, some beautiful contrasts. What is important is the fact that this person chose to focus on this subject in this way, based on their background and experience. It is aesthetic, but it's aesthetic at a different level. You know that there is a reason why the photograph was taken that way, that it was significant to the person who took it. If that comes across in the story that appears alongside it, then it can become a beautiful photo.

AL: It comes back to the issue of hierarchy and a kind of registration of authorship. I call myself a photographer, but I work mostly with other people's photographs. I think people who work with photographs always need to contextualise the means of production and the intentions and ambitions that informed their work, regardless of the kind of making involved.

ED: With regards to aesthetics and the methodology I use, the stories come before the photography. I trained the people I was working with in photography, in parallel with the development of other parts of the project. So, we were working together trying to comprehend our experiences and decide what it is we wanted to talk about and, by the point we were ready to start taking pictures, the women knew how. The middle section of *Open Shutters Iraq* is

No excuses now. Get out there and enjoy, come rain or shine.
© Sian Angus/DiversityInCare/PhotoVoice, 2013

I want to be a real mum.
© Tracey Sumner/DiversityInCare/PhotoVoice, 2013

Desta Getaneh, *Voices of Freedom*. PhotoVoice, 2014

made up of photographic essays, and they are all quite stylised, but they are stylised because those women had the intention to see their experience in a certain way. They chose to use photography in a certain way because that's how they wanted to use photography to communicate.

AL: There's also a dialogue between you and the subjects that takes place around editing the story and how you caption pictures.

ED: Absolutely, and I am currently thinking about how to make this process much more visible. The research and my role within it is often invisible. If we looked at participation in a graph, then, for example, my participation might appear much higher than that of others at the beginning, while others might have very little participation at the start and their participation would then go up or down, depending on how the work is structured.

AD: I think it's so important not to disguise it.

ED: Whenever I work I obviously look back and critique it and, in *Open Shutters Iraq*, I don't think I'm visible enough. I don't think its transparent enough in terms of the process. The work is a collaboration on so many different levels, with so many different people: the institution, the funder, the person who's making it or designing the workshop, and I am at the centre. That's why I don't mind calling myself the author. At the end of the day, it's not just working with the people who make the stories.

BB: Perhaps there's a practical issue here in terms of the photography book as a vehicle for some of these projects? To introduce that kind of critical self-reflexive element to the projects would require you to work outside some of the design conventions that have become fairly entrenched in photobook publishing, particularly in recent years.

NS: You can introduce a voice, which is what they did at Half Moon—they used tape recorders as well. That worked well with the moving image,

Tizalu Brahan, *Voices of Freedom*. PhotoVoice, 2014

Basilica of the Annunciation, Nazareth by Tizalu Brahan,
Voices of Freedom. PhotoVoice, 2014

Desta Getaneh, *Voices of Freedom*. PhotoVoice, 2014

where a voice was placed over changing stills. There is a potential continuity there between the 1970s and a kind of contemporary multimedia model in a way. I think that that's very effective. Then it moves it away from the gallery, the monograph, the newspaper, academia, you actually hear the people who are involved in these projects.

MD: There is a flipside to all of this found in a certain version of journalism, which sits at the blurry boundary between fact and fiction based on the mobilisation of all kinds of participants.

BB: So, I wonder where we situate the types of projects we have been discussing in relation to citizen journalism? For a writer such as Daniel Palmer, citizen journalism shares some important characteristics with 1970s community photography. How do you feel the supposed democratisation of media representation impacts on all this?

AL: I see digital platforms such as blogs and Facebook groups as tools I can use to enable the viewpoints of the participants to become more visible in the work. At the same time, I also feel they can be a valuable way to chart the process of making the work.

MD: I think the perceived democratisation of the media has been quite useful for what we do at PhotoVoice, because there is an increasing sense that people have the right to put their thoughts out there. This allows us to draw attention to those people that don't have that right because of their status in a society, or because their society hasn't developed to that stage and they don't have access to that technology. In either context, we have a really straightforward justification for why these people should be given the opportunity to speak out.

ED: But, again, I struggle with that point. People can't be given opportunity—they have to take it.

Authorship, Collaboration, Computation?

Into the Realm of Similar Images

with
ERICA SCOURTI

Text by
KATRINA SLUIS

Photographers may think they are bringing their own aesthetic, epistemological or political criteria to bear. They may set out to take artistic, scientific or political images for which the camera is only a means to an end. But what appear to be their criteria for going beyond the camera nevertheless remain subordinate to the camera's program. Vilém Flusser, *Towards a Philosophy of Photography*

I feel like everyone sort of has the same photos.

Hannah, a respondent in a 2008 Facebook study

In 2011, Google added a 'search by image' feature to its suite of search products. Capitalising on advances in computer recognition, the tool enabled users to find images with similar 'visual fingerprints' spread across the web. On Google's search blog, Johanna Wright, Director of Search Product Management, described its value as follows:

You might have an old vacation photo, but forgot the name of that beautiful beach. Typing [guy on a rocky path on a cliff with an island behind him] isn't exactly specific enough to help find your answer. So when words aren't as descriptive as the image, you can now search using the image itself.[1]

Being able to search 'visually' was the latest method through which one might overcome the fallibility of human memory in an age of accelerating data. Its launch presented Google as an indispensable aide, collaborator and confidante for your digital lifestyle. Or, as Google VP Marisa Meyer phrased it: 'Your best friend with instant access to all the world's facts and a photographic memory of everything you've seen and know.'[2] Through the magic of pattern-recognition algorithms, Google would be there to help you recall names and locations, and create novel vectors between your snapshots and billions of others in only milliseconds. By temporarily unifying groups of dispersed images hosted on remote web servers, the tool offered itself up as a kind of networked, protological vision machine. Just as image tagging had transformed Web 2.0 platforms, here was a technology that offered a new navigational paradigm for the image 'cloud'. But, whereas tagging was an important part of the social life of platforms such as Flickr, with 'reverse image search' it became possible to plot a course through a web of images using the ordering logic of the machine's gaze. Think your #srsly #cute #scottishfold #cat is unique? Think your enhanced high-dynamic-range photo of the Franz Josef glacier viewed from the altar window of Waiho church in the South Island of New Zealand is unique? Think again. The grouping, aggregating and tracking online of images 'visually' made it possible to discover images that were *just like yours*, and escape the image-language problem of previous archival taxonomies. >

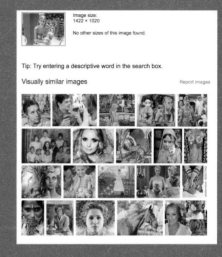

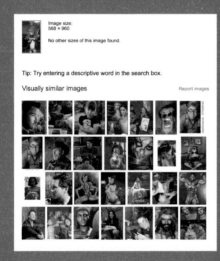

Authorship and Collective Labour

in an Image Cloud

Perhaps unsurprisingly, it was not in the potential imag(in)ing of collective memory but in the arena of rights management that Google's reverse image search was quickly co-opted by photographers. Professionals and amateurs alike praised the tool for its ability to track an image's reuse online in order to 'catch copyright crooks' and 'recover what is rightfully yours'. Rather than sending photographers into a spiral of angst around the cultural politics of reproduction, 'search by image' became the Holy Grail for a community intent on defending its authentic creativity against an information economy that valorises the real-time exchange of multiple, simultaneous, orphaned images.

But the question of how to be acknowledged as an author—with all the economic and social capital that entails—is not just limited to professional photographers in network culture. The pursuit of self-realisation through creative digital labour has been a defining feature of social media in an era characterised by hyper-individualism (observe the rise of the 'selfie') and hyper-consumption (observe the rise of the 'selfie, holding my new boutique pet'). Within neoliberal culture we are all invited to endlessly re-invent ourselves, turn our life into a work of art and, in the process, make ourselves transparent to software and to each other. How, then, might it be possible to be recognised as a unique individual with a creative voice when Instagram has made everyone's photos look the same?

In considering this paradox, it is worth returning to a question that has haunted photography since its inception: is photography a technology of reproduction or a tool for artistic expression? The problem with the latter, as critics point out, is that the collective labour that makes photographic reproduction possible (from design and marketing to manufacturing and display) is rendered invisible when the photograph is limited to a creative act originating in the mind of an individual photographer. And despite the increasing automation of photography, this model of modernist authorship persists in the rhetoric of consumer electronics manufacturers, museums, and university photography courses alike. But when the act of viewing, searching or tagging an image online potentially changes its visibility, velocity and legibility, the separation of author from audience, individual from crowd becomes extraneous. Not least because today's web architectures have become 'social machines' in which the boundaries between computations performed by machine logic and those that result from human sentiment are increasingly interwoven. >

Collaborating

with
Machines

It is precisely this meshwork of humans and non-humans, images and code that the artist Erica Scourti attends to in her practice. Setting out to test the limits of self-expression in a fully mediated culture, her work explores the tension between the desire to be (or believe oneself to be) authentic and singular within it. Subjecting her life to the gaze of the machine (and keenly aware of the implicit narcissism), Scourti has collaborated with security experts, software platforms, Googlebots and other network users in her search for self-knowledge. Informing her approach is an understanding that sharing the digital detritus of our lives may connect us to a host of interested and interesting unknown people, in ways that ultimately require us to be readable to others (and their non-human agents) too.

In *Life in AdWords* (2012–13), Scourti wrote and emailed her diary to her Gmail account over a year, collecting the keywords that Google had scanned and harvested for targeted advertisements. She read the results to her webcam wherever she happened to be that day, creating video portraits of her life as mined and understood by Google's algorithms. Rather than a document of authentic or quotidian experience, Scourti explains that her diary became a compilation of 'clusters of relevant ads, making visible the way we and our personal information are the product in the "free" Internet economy'. Hijacking and making visible the commercial exploitation of personal data, the project uses the intimate mode of the webcam confession in order to raise the question of whether there is any area of life that can't be assimilated and commodified through the power of computer analytics.

In approaching her commission for Brighton Photo Biennial 2014, Scourti sets out to discover what happens when statistical correlations are used to delineate existing links between things and direct relationships between people. Beginning with the specificity of her own personal memory—in the form of documents, love letters, snapshots and other ephemera—she uses Google's 'search by image' function to create a version of her own life through the discovery of thousands of other images that visually resemble it. Brought into this process is an array of network users who gain a temporary closeness

with Erica not through shared interests but through the statistical similarities determined by Google's VisualRank algorithm. Her investigation into the mediation of the self through software also has links to the increasingly popular paradigm of the statistically derived or quantified self—in which one's own identity makes sense as part of a wider demographic. With this in mind, Scourti asks us to consider how this tension between the individual and the collective be staged in relation to the images we capture and continuously share? What does it mean to open oneself up to metadata? What possibilities become available when you acknowledge software as a collaborator in the reflexive project of the self?

Scourti's work help to highlight the way that a photograph's value might not lie in the specificity of its content but in its legibility to machines and the data generated around it. Whilst photographers continue to demand control of their intellectual 'property', ownership and monetisation of the data that accumulates as a by-product of our collective creativity remain less contested. This is, of course, what Getty understood when it decided to give away its image assets for 'free'—with the condition that we permit it to harvest information about the photograph's use. This reflects a paradigm shift in which there is less value to be extracted from individual images than from the relations between them. These relations tell us much about audience sentiment, patterns of consumption and potential future demand for images. The situation has wider implications for culture, as data-driven decision-making becomes the latest business meme to cross over into UK arts policy. One wonders if, in the future, it will be Getty and not the gallery that will serve as an example of what an audience-responsive, market-driven, image-serving organisation might look like in tune with the public's cultural desires.

1   Google: Inside Search, 'Search by text, voice, or image', http://insidesearch.blogspot.co.uk/2011/06/search-by-text-voice-or-image.html (18 June 2014).

2   Google: Official Blog, 'The future of search', http://googleblog.blogspot.co.uk/2008/09/future-of-search.html (18 June 2014).

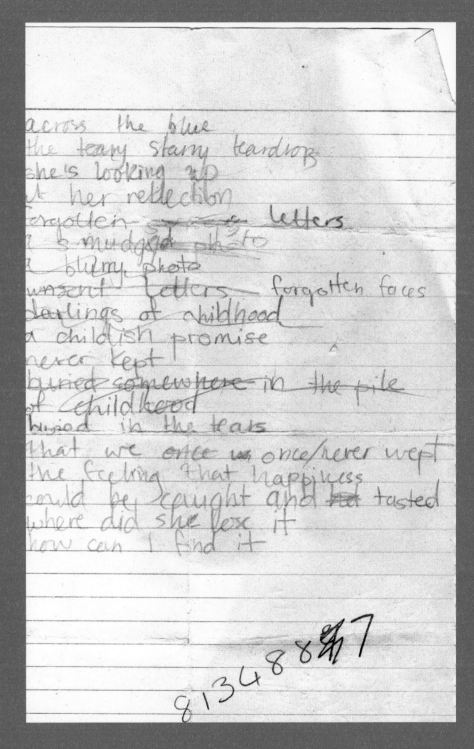

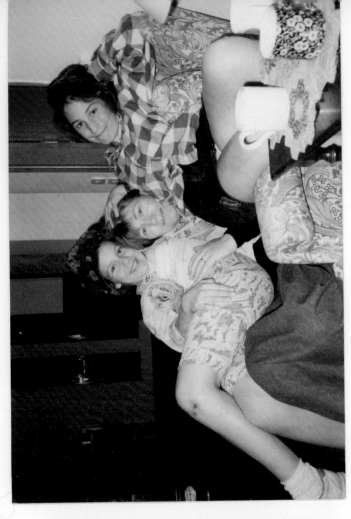

Amateur Photographic Communities.

Left: Unknown photographer, Cambridge and Bethnal Green boys at camp in Greatstones with cameras, 1937. Tower Hamlets Local History and Archives, S/NCB/2/1/1, with permission from Cambridge and Bethnal Green Old Boys' Club

Below: Unknown photographer, Cambridge and Bethnal Green Boys' Club outing, c. 1935–40. Tower Hamlets Local History and Archives, S/NCB/2/1/1, with permission from Cambridge and Bethnal Green Old Boys' Club

Real
and
Imagined

JULIET BAILLIE

in
conversation
with

ANNEBELLA
POLLEN

Juliet Baillie: How have issues of collaboration and community played out in your work on amateur photography?

Annebella Pollen: I have a longstanding interest in amateur photographic practices, addressed through a range of historical case studies. In particular, I spent some years analysing 55,000 photographs taken on a single day in 1987 for a national charity fundraising project called *One Day for Life*. This project used the entry fees from an ambitious photographic competition as a means of securing large-scale charitable participation. It resulted in a best-selling photographic book and, later, an archive of the entire collection of submitted prints. The project was initially interesting to me because it offered a means of accessing amateur photographs on a scale rarely possible in the pre-digital period. It also allowed me to see how judgements about good and bad photographs played out through a complex selection and editorial process.

I've since developed this work to explore what I call mass participation photography. By this, I mean the popular photographic projects that are frequently structured around a life-in-a-day model. These have a long history, but have become increasingly popular with the advent of digital and networked photography. Large numbers of, usually, amateur photographers are enlisted to create collective photographic events that variously function as time capsules, portraits of a nation, global snapshots of daily life and so on. These kinds of projects clearly intersect with the theme of collaboration, as they often seek to use photography to build temporary communities around collective identities, shared causes and group activities.

JB: My own work over the past few years has been concerned with skilled amateur photography, looking at the photographic practices of camera club members, particularly in 1930s London. Although I am focusing on a different time and context to you, I am also interested in examining the photographs produced by amateur photographers and, particularly, the role their interactions with each other played in shaping their practices. The informal photographic clubs built communities of photographic activity and participation. But they also existed within a broader network of clubs and federations—a broader community, in a sense—that governed, or at the very least influenced, the activities of individual members.

AP: Ideas of collaboration also intersect with our shared work around the reconsideration of amateur photography,

conducted for the National Media Museum. Several of the essays we commissioned closely examine—and take seriously—amateur photographic practices, in terms of what they mean to their participants, rather than simply evaluating the aesthetic or technical inadequacies of sometimes less-than-perfect amateur photographs. In the work of Jonas Larsen on tourist photography, Peter Buse on the photographic communities developed in the pages of photography magazines and, most of all, Elizabeth Edwards on Edwardian photographers' leisure excursions, we encounter efforts to explore how communities are created and performed through collective photographic acts that articulate shared values.

This approach requires an understanding of photography as a complex social and cultural practice that precedes (and often exceeds) the resulting images. In so much photographic analysis, the final photograph is the privileged central focus, while the conditions of its production can be demoted to mere context. Do you think this is a valid way of approaching the practices of a camera club? Should we be thinking about the social production of the photographs—achieved through collective participation, discussion and judgement—as much as the photographs themselves?

Box 19, non-shortlisted photographs, One Day for Life photography collection, Mass-Observation Archive, University of Sussex. Photograph by Annebella Pollen, 2010

Photograph submitted to One Day for Life
photographic competition, 1987, by an anony-
mous photographer, showing One Day for
Life publicity. Box 2, Shortlisted photographs,
One Day for Life photography collection.
With permission of the Trustees of the Mass-
Observation Archive, University of Sussex

JB: Yes, I think it is important, if not crucial, to consider amateur photographic practices in this way.

AP: Only amateur photographic practices?

JB: No, I suppose all photographic practice
should be considered in this way. But I think it is
particularly important in the case of amateurs,
due to the tendency for their photographs to be
seen as hapless or lacking in originality in light
of models of scholarship based on the conventions of art history. In reality, skill or originality
might not necessarily be central to their purpose. Skill was central to camera clubs but, in
some respects, the photographs produced in
this context could be considered straightforward reflections of the social interaction that
was part of amateur photography's function as
a leisure activity. Whether it was reading photographic magazines, attending club meet-
ings, going on excursions, visiting or exhibiting
in photographic salons, all of these activities
fed into a particular approach to photography
that was seen in camera clubs at the time. This
sociability, and its shaping effects, was funda-
mental to the practice of photography in these
clubs, which were dominated by a kind of pictorial
photography, predicated on a narrow field of aesthetics, and the production of fine prints.

AP: It is interesting that you use the term 'sociability', because the group projects that I have been examining are
rather different in that sense. With events such as One
Day for Life, mentioned above, or more recent global collective media projects such as One Day on Earth (2010),
the YouTube-generated Life in a Day (2011) or the A Day
in the World project (2012), the thousands, even tens of
thousands, of participants rarely, if ever, meet. Rather,
individual contributors respond to a broad and inclusive
invitation to participate and are therefore constituted as a
photographic community only through their participation.

In a way, this shares many characteristics with Benedict Anderson's famous theories of national identity as an
imagined community. Members of any nation will rarely
meet, but they are brought into collective relationships
by national practices, and experience what he calls 'deep
horizontal comradeship'. For many contributors to the
photographic events that I have studied, it is the act of collaboration in a project that is much larger than themselves
that creates the meaningful experience. It is less about
their identity as a photographer or their individual submis-
sion, more about the part that their photography plays in a
collective vision. If there's a sense that a photograph can
go beyond the personal circumstances that generated
it into some sort of larger conversation, then a sense of
group identity and even belonging can be forged. >

JB: What do you think is it about photography that lends itself to these kinds of community-building projects?

AP: First and foremost, it is no doubt because photography is popularly seen as an accessible and democratic medium. But I also think that photographs, with all of their inbuilt ambiguity, lend themselves nicely to symbolic projects. A photograph of your child can become a photograph about something more abstract, such as the concept of childhood, in another context where the impetus may be to create a national portrait or make a historical statement. The ease of new technology and photography's supposed universal legibility can also make it adaptable to collective and, increasingly, globally ambitious projects that seek to harness the mass ownership of cameras and the mass practice of photography. Their newly networked status also facilitates collective projects that would be logistically complex, if not impossible, in analogue and pre-internet formats.

But we have begun to talk freely about photographic communities here—whether they be 1930s camera clubs or 21st-century global photographic events—without actually saying what we understand 'community' to mean. Clearly, the demographic make-up of any community matters as much as the fact that photography is shaped by collective decision-making. Who are the communities that take part in club activities, in terms of your work?

Unknown photographer, Croydon Camera Club outing by boat, c. 1925. Croydon Camera Club Archive

JB: When I started looking at this area, it seemed as though all the clubs were going to be very middle class: people, mainly men, with disposable income, who had a bit of leisure time to spend tinkering around with cameras and photographic equipment, meeting up in the church hall once a week to chat about it. Those kinds of photographers did make up a large proportion of what I found, although their relationship with photography was more nuanced than the stereotypes suggest, and their sense of community and group identity was strong.

What was especially interesting for me, though, was to discover the clubs that didn't fit that mould. In the East End of London, for example, Cambridge and Bethnal Green Boys' Club—a club where teenage boys could go after school or work to take part in a kind of enlivening or productive leisure—had a photographic section and ultimately a photographic club. Despite having relatively basic cameras, they had photography lessons and outings and produced photographs for exhibitions.

Life in a Day film poster

AP: That's interesting. Who organised those kinds of activities? Did they come from the boys' own interests or was there a sense that photography might be a way of inculcating improving moral values? That is, was this a community that was shaped from above or from within?

JB: There was a combination of activity, some of which was of their own making, but also from above, being influenced by their teacher at Cambridge and Bethnal Green Boys' Club and wider associations for Boys' Clubs at the time. Their photographic activity fitted with the rhetoric around leisure between the wars, which encouraged using free time for self-improvement. Whether you worked in a factory or as an accountant, monotony was considered conducive to exhaustion, boredom and seeking improper leisure pursuits. There was a fear, as writer Lawrence Pearsall Jacks noted at the time, that 'ready-made pleasures' and 'entertainment in which the sex flavour is uppermost' (!) would prevail. Engaged and productive leisure, on the other hand, could help to create better citizens and build community.

As an example, the Star and Garter Home was a residential home in Richmond for wounded soldiers, veterans of the First World War, many of whom were paraplegics. It had a camera club from the early 1920s, and there is a very real sense that it helped these soldiers to be a community in themselves, but also to be part of the local community. They went on trips, interacted with other local camera clubs and even printed photographs commercially. There is a sense that photography was part of their rehabilitation and also allowed them to be productive members of society.

AP: The idea of photographic engagement as a form of civic identity-building is also important to many of the projects I have studied. Many of these seek to use photography as a vehicle for other causes, whether this is as nebulous a concept as 'raising awareness', fostering a sense of 'global citizenship' or in providing an effective and imaginative means of raising funds. The last was particularly true of 1980s and 1990s photography projects in aid of cancer research or heart disease charities. Others are envisaged as historical repositories. The History Channel, for example, organised *Photos for the Future* projects around the time of the millennium in order to make a kind of time capsule, and there were very many 'people's photography' projects clustered around the turn of the 21st century that used photography as a means of cementing local or national identity.

Some of these were ultimately commercial ventures that may well have paid mere lip service to some of the more abstract and wholesome concepts of community engagement. Very few are community photography projects in the sense that some of the radical 'committed photography' projects of the 1970s aimed to be. But participants nonetheless attribute powerful personal and public meaning to their participation. That's worth taking seriously, and it moves the debate on from fairly circular arguments about the political effectiveness of such projects. Photography can't change the world.

One of the things that is interesting is that, sometimes, little reference to the sociable production of knowledge—the sense of community participation or the performance of citizenship—is visible in the surface of the resulting

A Day.org global digital exhibition in London, 15 May 2012

print. I think this raises some complex questions, both methodological and philosophical. Is this something that you observed in relation to camera club photographs from the 1930s? It is certainly something that I have noticed in my work. Participation as a feeling is hard to picture, unless you literally take a photograph of multiple people holding cameras (as some meta-photographers in these projects do).

JB: I have come across some really fantastic photographs of club members posing with their cameras. Those pictures always get a good reaction—there is something irresistible about them—but they also show how these photographers identify themselves as a certain kind of photographer, often with a certain kind of camera. They often prefer to look through the lens of their own camera rather than directly at the photographer making the exposure.

In the case of camera club photography, the participation and sociality of the activity is literally inscribed in the surface of the print. Photography in the clubs I studied was quite regimented. The set-up of the clubs, and the wider networks to which they belonged, meant that the aesthetics of the photographs were really quite narrow—they continued to be inspired, to some degree, by turn of the century pictorialism. What I found to be most significant to this kind of photography was the print as a showcase of craftsmanship and technical skill. The community worked together, sharing hints and tips that would make their photography technically better and help them to produce a fine print. The same judges were used for many competitions and exhibitions, and you could say that a formula developed for how these photographs looked and the quality of finish that was expected. Competition amongst peers was viewed as productive in this respect.

AP: Is that incompatible with community, then? Competition sounds like photographers working against one another rather than coming together.

JB: I suppose it does sound that way but, actually, it was a means of encouraging photographers to be active in their hobby, to really participate, and to develop the skills that club membership supported. A club would be better represented in inter-club competitions if members were encouraged to compete with each other. Ultimately, they would improve their craft. I could turn the same question back to you. The events that you examine are sometimes structured as competitions. Does this conflict with their simultaneous attempts to build a photographic community?

AP: Great question! It's tricky. I think perhaps there's an idealised gloss on all of the terms we are using here: community, collaboration and participation. They all seem to embody such deeply wholesome values that competition can easily be placed in opposition. In practice, the terms are not mutually exclusive. While both have a shaping effect on the content produced, many participants who I interviewed in my research on *One Day for Life* took the position of 'it's not the winning, it's the taking part'. In any case, there are often multiple reasons for people to take part in these kinds of events. For some, winning the competition and getting their photo seen was all. For others, charitable donation, a sense of national pride (or critique) or even a sense of keen historical consciousness prompted their participation.

ADay.org global digital exhibition in London, 15 May 2012

Croydon Camera Club, 'Club Members circa 1940s.
From left to right: Morgan; Beeston; Witty; Spackman.
Taken at the club meeting rooms "The Studio",
Edridge Road'. Photograph probably by P. H. Mason
of 181 Brighton Road, South Croydon

Most participants enjoy photography, and believe that it can play a distinctively expressive role, but photography is often only part of the appeal. In terms of competition, even in collective photographic events that are not consciously constructed in that way, some element of selection usually takes place in the resulting book, film, exhibition or web pages. This necessarily positions some photographs as more visually appealing, emblematic or otherwise more highly valued than others; the resulting public face of community photography projects is managed and filtered.

> JB: There is certainly a sense that competing with each other in the club, and more broadly with other amateur photographers, helped to create a cohesive sense of identity, as skilled photographers. I found very little evidence of dissenters in the camera club community. In one case, a club member wrote some satirical articles that mocked stereotypical club photography and photographers—deeming them to be technically obsessed 'old bores'—but he was stopped by the club committee. It may be that conflict of that sort was not generally recorded!

AP: I did find plentiful examples of participants who aimed to go against the celebratory grain of their mass-photographic projects. Interestingly, they still take part, but use the opportunity to make a critical statement with their photograph. The emphasis on national celebration, for example, that was so prevalent in *One Day for Life* caused concern for those who felt marginalised or excluded from its national boundaries or political agendas, and this resulted in a range of fascinating, dissenting images that stick two fingers up or show modern life at its dirty, materialistic worst. They want to show a different kind of 'we'.

More generally, I think it is all too easy to be cynical about the limits of photographic participation, as if only those projects that are fully and transparently collectively devised, conducted, edited, circulated and received can achieve the gold standard. In practice, many collective projects that involve a degree of collaboration and participation may not be so democratically articulated or carried through, and editorial boards, competition judges, curators and others may all play a part in shaping and controlling the meaning and outcome of content generated through collective amateur and voluntary contribution. The term 'community' is also open to critique, not least when it is used in some dubious political contexts. We could argue that photographic communities that only exist as symbolic entities—formed around a short-lived collective event or activity—are rhetorical figments rather than actual communities. But such symbolic communities can produce a powerful sense of belonging, even when they are themselves contrived. Collective identity may well be imagined, as Anderson and other scholars have indicated, but it is not *imaginary*. If individual actors believe in it, it is socially real and has important consequences.

Close Ties: The Railway Station as a Hub of photographic Exchange

JENNIFER TUCKER

These cathedrals of the new humanities are the meeting points of nations, the centre where all converges, the nucleus of the huge stars whose iron rays stretch out to the ends of the earth.

Pierre Jules Théophile Gautier [1]

'Stations are the cathedrals of our century', proposed an anonymous contributor to *The Building News* in 1875. As monasteries and cathedrals were to the 13th century, so railway terminals and hotels were to the 19th. The essay went on to propose that cathedrals and stations were the only truly representative buildings that those centuries possessed. [2]

Railway stations invited comparison with cathedrals because both the station and the cathedral symbolised important cultural preoccupations and moral values of their age. As a point of transit, both formed the central node in a network of mobility and institutional power, providing a massive physical structure that also carried great symbolic significance. The Gothic cathedral and the Victorian railway terminus were similar to each other in another way: as primary focal points of artistic and engineering activity, both served as cultural meeting points for the intellectual and cultural networks that helped formulate the visual processes, techniques and values of their periods.

Photography's history in the first century after its invention in 1839 offers a record of the railway station's importance as a new source of photographic collaboration, and a window through which to glimpse, at least for a moment, the connections, relationships and ordinary friendships that structured early photographic interests, too often overlooked by dominant photographic studies, which emphasise individual photographers working in isolation. Even the physical construction of the railway lines provided artists and engineers with new modes of visual representation. Praising the contribution of photography to the building of the rail infrastructure of the British Empire in a speech delivered to the British Association for the Advancement of Science in 1858, the British palaeontologist Richard Owen boasted that 'The engineer at home can ascertain, by photographs transmitted by successive mails, the weekly progress, brick by brick, board by board, nail by nail, of the most complex works on the Indian or other remote railroads.' [3]

Albumen photograph, c. 1868, showing the construction of the roof of St Pancras station, in *Photographs of the Works in Progress of the Midland Railway-Extension to London* (two volumes), c. 1867–68. (Photograph album (1988-8759), vol. 2, image reference 1086/80, National Railway Museum, York)

An album of photographs commissioned by the Midland Railway to document the construction of London's St Pancras station, 1867–68, is a record of both engineering virtuosity and social achievement. [4] A photograph of the construction of the roof of St Pancras station records a stage in the progress of the building of the Midland Railway extension in London. [5] Completed by the engineer William Henry Barlow in 1868, the train shed was the largest single-span structure built up to that time. The way in which the St Pancras station architecture borrowed explicitly from the architecture of a Gothic cathedral may be seen in the vaulted roof, which not only unified the space and protected travellers from the elements but also permitted the dispersal of smoke from trains.

An albumen photograph of a geological cutting from a railroad construction near Leeds in 1890 shows the way in which the Victorian excavation of geological beds for modern railway construction provided unique opportunities for digging beneath the surface in order to visualise the traces of a deep past. Scientists in the Geological Photography Section of the British Association for the Advancement of Science requested help in the 1880s from amateur photographers to compile a documentary record of England's sedimentary traces, instructing them in how to take photographs that would contribute to scientific geological knowledge. Armed with cameras and standard observation forms, many members of camera clubs headed for their nearest railway building site. >

W. H. Fox, dry-plate gelatine photograph of a rail
cutting near Leeds, taken 1 January 1890. (BAAS
Geological Photographs, accession No. P231865,
Royal Geological Survey, Nottingham)

One such photograph, by amateur geologist and photographer W. H. Fox of York on New Year's Day 1890 using the gelatine dry-plate process, shows a sharp cut in the land that was made by civil engineers in the process of excavating a railway bed in a small farming town in North Yorkshire. The photograph was taken for inclusion in an album compiled by the British Association for the Advancement of Science's Geological Photographs Section using pictures solicited from photographers across the British Isles. It juxtaposes two scenes of time: first, the horizontal layers of flint shown in chalk formations that the process of building the new railway made visible to the eye; second, the lines of the railway that powerfully direct the eye into the distance.[6]

Photographs facilitated a new, industrial notion of disciplined time and, in this specific example, also placed the viewer in a previously unseen ancient geological landscape. If medieval choirs filled European cathedrals with sound, 'the immense and distant sound of time' was traced 600 years later through rail travel. So wrote American writer Thomas Wolfe in his laudatory prose poem about the railway station published in 1940:

> Few buildings are vast enough
> To hold the sound of time
> And now it seemed to him
> That there was a superb fitness in the fact
> That the one which held it better than all others
> Should be a railroad station.
> For here, as nowhere else on earth,
> Men were brought together for a moment
> At the beginning or end
> Of their innumerable journeys.[7]

As official rail photography grew in importance and the railway's publicity machines became more sophisticated, amateur photographers continued to flock to rail stations to photograph moving trains and other phenomena expressive of the new age of movement. Members of Britain's prestigious Railway Photographic Society, formed in 1922, circulated their prints to others in the club. Galvanised (and sometimes stung) by the feedback they received about their photographs, they sought to elevate the standard of railway photography by sharing and mproving its techniques. Composition, definition and impression of scale mattered for these rail photographers. 'I am afraid this doesn't appeal to me. I quite appreciate the conditions, and that it was a "special" train, but I would like to see a shot from this viewpoint on a clear day', wrote a member in a typical report in the 1940s. Another observed that a photograph had a 'very nice pictorial effort'—'*made* by the steam effects'. Above all, they strove to capture photographically what they saw as railway travel's special 'atmosphere'.[8]

From the late 1930s, an Anglican deacon (and, later, a canon), Eric Treacy, sought to put rail photography on a new footing by making images that captured what he called the 'spirit' of the railways. A long-time member of the Railway Photographic Society, Treacy (or 'the footplate bishop', as he became widely known) published rail photographs in various magazines during the 1930s, and published his first book of images in 1946, after serving as a military chaplain during the Second World War. He came to question the value of an uncompromising documentary approach to photographic train portraiture, expressing his belief that 'it should be possible to place the train in relation to the landscape so that the result is a picture rather than a mere photographic record':

> I am a loyal member of the Railway Photographic Society, but that does not prevent me from levelling a friendly criticism at the Society. I feel that they have done much to standardise our conception of railway photography. Most of the leading photographers belong to the R.P.S. [Royal Photographic Society], and have therefore made their pictures with an eye to the criticisms of their fellow members—with the result that the aim has too often been to produce a flawless portrait of a train.[9]

To introduce a note of variety ('to capture more side than one of the railway scene'), he enlisted the help of others:

> Recently I took a friend of mine who is an F.R.P.S.[10] photographing on the railway and he was ecstatic at the artistic possibilities of the railway setting. Immediately, he saw possibilities that I had never dreamt of: simply because I was in a rut and he came to it with the eye of an artist.

Because his parish in Edge Hill, near Liverpool Lime Street Station, encompassed a large locomotive depot, Treacy came to know many of the men who worked on the railroad. His appreciation of this wider aspect of the railway and its workers may be seen clearly in several of his photographs in which signalmen, engineers or track repairers helped him achieve balance and composition in his picture, in marked contrast to the work of most other railway photographers, many of whom tended to see such incursions as distracting.[11] On some occasions, especially hot summer days when steam was often harder to generate, help would take the form of 'smoke by arrangement'—a shovelful of coal tossed by the fireman into the firebox at just the right time could make all the difference to a picture. >

Eric Treacy, photograph of a steam locomotive bound for London, c. early 1950, capturing the movement of a train exiting Liverpool Lime Street Station with a puff of smoke. (The Treacy Collection (#1032310l), National Railway Museum, York)

1   Cited in Jeffrey Richards and John M. Mackenzie, *The Railway Station: A Social History* (London: Faber and Faber, 1986), p. 3.

2   *The Building News* (1875). See esp. Nikolaus Pevsner, *Pioneers of Modern Design: Frank William Morris to Walter Gropius* (New Haven, CT: Yale University Press, 2005), p. 72.

3   'The British Association for the Advancement of Science', *Photographic News* (1858), Oct. 8, p. 49.

4   According to architectural historian Neil Levine, a photograph taken in 1852 of the Bibliothèque Sainte-Geneviève by the Bisson Frères is very likely the first commissioned photograph of a contemporary building. See Neil Levine, 'The template of photography in 19th century architectural representation', *Journal of the Society of Architectural Historians* (2012), vol. 71, No. 3, pp. 306–331.

5   Photograph album, *Photographs of the Works in Progress of the Midland Railway-Extension to London* (two volumes), c. 1867–68, National Railway Museum, York (1998-8759). Two photographers associated with the album have been identified as John Baker Pyne Junior, whose embossed stamp records that he was a photographer based at 167 Prince of Wales' Road in Haverstock Hill, London NW. According to Michael Pritchard's online '*Directory of London Photographers, 1841–1908*', he was active from 1858 to 1878. His father, who had the same name, was vice-president of the Society of British Artists. Another was J. Ward, Photographer, of 78 Euston Road, London, who according to Pritchard was active between 1866 and 1871.

6   The photograph was used at the time by the British Association to characterise the geological 'Middle Chalk' formation (later described as the 'Welton Chalk Formation.') In Yorkshire, as shown here, the underlying stratum has the highest concentration of flints.

7   Thomas Wolfe, *You Can't Go Home Again* (New York: Harper, 1940), p. 48. The train was the most pervasive symbol in Thomas Wolfe's works. See Richard Walser, 'Thomas Wolfe's train as symbol', *Southern Literary Journal* (1988), vol. 21, No. 1, pp. 3–14.

8   Railway Photographic Society Folios (ALS5/14/D/1 CCB Herbert), National Railway Museum, York. The Railway Photographic Society lasted into the early 1970s, although the circulation of prints for criticism was in decline by then.

9   Eric Treacy, *Still More of My Best Railway Photographs* (London: Ian Allan, 1948), vol. 13, p. 4.

10 Fellow of the Royal Photographic Society.

11 A memorial to Treacy's life in railway photography is commemorated with a plaque at Appleby station, where he died from a heart attack in 1978 while waiting to photograph the *Evening Star* on a steam special. The Treacy Collection of 12,000 photographs forms part of the National Railway Museum's archive of over 1.5 million images. With kind thanks to Ed Bartholomew, Curator of Image and Sound Collections, National Railway Museum, York, for his assistance with this research.

Photographic Collaboration in Anthropology, Past and Present

Past and Present

ELIZABETH EDWARDS

HAIDY GEISMAR

CHRISTOPHER MORTON

When photography and anthropology emerged, mid-19th century, they were, in Chris Pinney's words, immediately 'entangled'.[1] Both were recognised as nascent sciences of mankind, as modes of inscription that were able to shed empirical light on the diversity, and universal qualities, of human existence. Much has been written about photography's immediate co-option into anthropological theories of race, and its use as a tool of measurement and comparative analysis, which speaks to broader understandings of photography as objective and evidential. However, a second strand of photographic theory—the nature of photography as a collaborative and subjective medium, co-produced between the technology itself, the photographer and the photographed—has also resonated with anthropological practice since the beginning.

In these brief meditations, three anthropologists working with photography have each chosen images that speak to the lengthy history of anthropological photography and the nature of collaboration. They are all members of the Royal Anthropological Institute's photography committee, responsible for both stewarding the institute's extensive photographic collections and for generating productive dialogues regarding the ongoing role of photography in anthropology and vice versa. These three meditations on collaboration indicate how the historical archive of anthropological photographs has been co-opted into local meanings, and created new pathways to engage with difficult histories. They also demonstrate that the multivalent capacity of photography, and its ability to both inscribe scientific projects and forge deeply personal relationships, has been present from the very beginning. These comments all focus on the relationship of indigenous people in the present day to the archive of anthropological photographs. Anthropologists in the present day continue to use photography as both a collaborative research method and an exploratory practice, creatively linking people and place, and forging new archives as well as circuits for the exchange of photographic images. >

Elizabeth Edwards

Some time in 1898 a group of Cambridge academics and a group of Torres Strait Islanders were messing about with a camera. This episode resulted in one of the 'iconic' images of the history of anthropology, depicting the members of the Cambridge Expedition to the Torres Strait: leader Alfred Cort Haddon (seated), W. H. R. Rivers Charles Seligman, Sidney Ray, a London school master with a special knowledge of Melanesian languages, and Anthony Wilkin (responsible for the expeditions photography). However, the photograph was probably taken by an islander, in all likelihood one of the four men who appear in a companion, and less-well-known image (see p.178): Gizu (seated) Waria, Peter and Tom.

This second photograph was made a few minutes later—note the almost identical shadows but the greater number of footprints in the sand, made as the groups swapped position. But, significantly, it self-consciously mirrors the pose and demeanour of the other as a commanding statement of presence. The camera had passed from expedition hands to Islander hands and back again.

This pair of photographs is symbolic of the range of photographic sociability, collaboration and exchange that marked cross-cultural relations on Mabuyag in 1898. It points to the closeness of collaboration in the production of ethnographic knowledge. There has been a long debate on the extent to which those subject to anthropological study can write themselves into the ethnographies of them. The Torres Strait expedition worked with a group of senior men, such as Gizu, who acted as intermediaries, interpreters when necessary, friends and, on occasion, gatekeepers who decided how much secret knowledge could be divulged to the anthropologists and under what conditions. Collaboration was therefore not simply a way of acquiring anthropological knowledge but, from the Islander perspective, a way of controlling and maintaining ownership of that knowledge, even within the asymmetries of colonial relationships.

Photography was at the heart of this tightly negotiated ethnographic and social reciprocity. The senior men re-enacted major cultural practices for the expedition's camera in ways that complicate the relations of power and authorship. Indeed, collaborating with the aims of the expedition, however alien they might have felt to Islanders, was seen as an opportunity to record practices that they fully knew were under threat. These photographs stand for that complex relationship. In return, the expedition serviced the photographic desires of local people. They acted as wedding photographer and family photographic 'studio', even taking post-mortem photographs at the request of the family when a baby died.

The expedition also showed lantern slides of photographs taken by Haddon on an earlier visit in 1888. Although by 1898 the Torres Strait Islanders were familiar with lantern slide shows because of the strong presence of missionaries who used them as a staple of mission instruction, the expedition lantern slide shows were of a different order. The shows were, in effect, about island history and personal histories. They were so wildly popular that they had to be repeated night after night. Significantly, they were absorbed into local exchange systems as people brought food gifts to the lantern slide shows. This exchange of bananas and coconuts for lantern slides, like the moment of messing about with a camera on Mabuyag in 1898, positions photographs as both facilitators and symbols of complex collaborative relationships. While asymmetries of power, photographic control and voice imbricate these images at every level, at the same time their existence, and that of other expedition photographs, complicates the nature of the relationships from which they emerged, laying the foundations for ongoing collaborative work in the 21st century. Another member of our photographic committee, Anita Herle, as the curator responsible for the Haddon Collection in the Cambridge Museum of Archaeology and Anthropology, has made numerous visits to the Torres Strait and received many delegations of visiting Torres Strait Islanders in Cambridge.

The impetus for this ongoing collaboration comes not just from the changing landscape of museum practice but also from the Torres Strait. Long after the expedition returned home, Haddon was responding to requests for photographs from Islanders. In June 1901 he received a letter, via a pearler named Cowling, from Tommy, a Torres Strait man who had worked closely with the expedition: 'Tommy wants me to ask you to send him a photo of his family that you took as one of his daughters is dead, and he wants to look at her again.' >

Alfred Cort Haddon and the members of the Cambridge Expedition to the
Torres Strait, 1898. Image courtesy of Cambridge Museum of Archaeology
and Anthropology

Gizu, Waria, Peter and Tom photographed during the
Cambridge Expedition to the Torres Strait, 1898. Image courtesy
of Cambridge Museum of Archaeology and Anthropology

Christopher Morton

Whilst in Adelaide in August 2013 as part of a project on Australian Aboriginal photographic histories,[2] I was introduced to Lynnette Wanganeen, a descendant of the subject of an early Australian Aboriginal portrait in the Pitt Rivers Museum in Oxford, where I curate the photographic collection. The portrait in question is of James Wanganeen, who was an Aboriginal member of the Poonindie Mission in Port Lincoln, South Australia. I was delighted to be able to present Lynnette with a print of both this portrait, as well as one of James with his third wife, Mary Jane, and to speak at length to her about James and what having copies of the portraits meant to the family. The story of how I got to meet Lynnette is a great example of international collaboration.

The Oxford print is part of a set of images donated by the estate of Henry Wentworth Dyke Acland (1815–1900) after his death, half of which are portraits of missionised Aboriginal people, and the other half studio images of Aboriginal people in 'traditional' dress. It has all the hallmarks of a 'before-and-after' set of images compiled by a cleric to illustrate the work of the church in South Australia. Research continues into why Acland possessed this set of portraits, which perhaps relates to his connections with leading church figures in South Australia.

Portrait of James Wanganeen.
© Pitt Rivers Museum, University of Oxford

Portrait of James Wanganeen and Mary Jane.
© Pitt Rivers Museum, University of Oxford

The caption under the Oxford portrait reads 'Wongannin, aged 25', and it is believed that James Wanganeen's original name may have been Wanganni. He was an Upper Murray Maraura man born around 1836 who is thought to have left his home as a young boy after unrest in the community, and attended the Aboriginal school in Adelaide. However, when the school closed down in 1852, he was sent to the Poonindie Mission, which had been recently established by Archdeacon Mathew Hale.

As part of her research into the Pitt Rivers Museum collection in 2010, my collaborator Jane Lydon had contacted Adelaide historian Tom Gara, who assisted with the identification of 'Wongannin' as James Wanganeen. Jane then managed to contact James's descendent Lynnette Wanganeen and send her the Oxford portrait of James.

Coincidentally, in December 2011, Pauline Cockrill from the History Trust of South Australia had been on a visit to local museums in Port Lincoln when she spotted some daguerreotypes of Aboriginal people at the Mill Cottage Museum. Recognising their potential importance as among the earliest images of indigenous people in South Australia, Pauline took them back to Adelaide for conservation and further research. >

When a group of local experts was assembled to examine the daguerreotypes in Adelaide in February 2012, Tom Gara was among them. Having recently researched the Oxford portrait, Tom immediately recognised one of the daguerreotypes as another portrait of James Wanganeen. After hearing about the discovery of the daguerreotypes at Mill Cottage, Jane then put Pauline Cockrill in touch with Lynnette, who was invited to come and see the daguerreotype of her ancestor and to travel to Port Lincoln to see the portrait placed back on display.

A year and a half later, Pauline Cockrill and I are waiting outside the Old Lion Hotel in Adelaide, with two modern print copies of the Oxford portraits to give to Lynnette, made for me by the museum's photographer. When she arrives, we share a coffee next to a busy crossroads and talk about the photographs, the coincidences and the research networks that have brought us together. Lynnette is visibly moved to hold a copy of the portrait that was the key to identifying this man as James Wanganeen—no longer an anonymous Aboriginal sitter for an Adelaide studio photographer. She speaks in particular about the spiritual connections she feels across the generations.

Points of reconnection between archives and communities like this are part and parcel of the research process in museum anthropology these days. Ethnographic museums have been rethinking themselves as 'contact zones' between curators and indigenous communities for many years,[3] and the more symmetrical form of research collaboration that this necessarily involves has become central to rethinking the concept of the modern ethnographic museum.[4] The return of James Wanganeen was more than the institutional gifting of a reproduction photograph to a descendent: rather, it encompassed a much wider collaborative research process in which documentation in an Oxford archive held the key to understanding a local collection in Australia, and included insights from numerous international scholars.

Haidy Geismar

This photograph is one of my own, taken as part of a lengthy research project that reunited the people of the small islands of Malakula (part of the contemporary nation-state of Vanuatu) with the photographs made there in 1914–15 by the anthropologist John Layard. During the course of about six years I returned three times to the small islands of Atchin and Vao, each time carrying copies of the images, and different kinds of information about them, as I discovered the original captions in an American archive, or as I put more of my own archival research together. The project was an extended collaboration between the Cambridge Museum and the Vanuatu Cultural Centre (VCC) and National Museum. This research was published in the form of two books: a full length academic monograph and a smaller volume, translated into Bislama, the national creole of Vanuatu, 1,000 copies of which were distributed across the country for free.[5]

The project was explicitly formed to encourage people from Vanuatu to participate in the process of documenting and reflecting upon their own history, as well as to actively participate in museum projects and archival research around collections originally made within their own communities. The movement of photographic images in this particular research context not only facilitated a broader sense of reconnection between 'source communities' and museum collections but affirmed the active role of photographs in contemporary imaginings of the past in Vanuatu as well as within the work of anthropologists.

The VCC and its National Museum have played a central role in the activation of contemporary relationships to historical images in Vanuatu, in large part through the social research projects that the VCC organises and endorses. Aural and visual recording, collecting, archiving and broadcasting is one of the most vital parts of VCC practice, making research accessible throughout the archipelago. The National Film and Sound Unit has a state-of-the-art recording studio that produces television programmes, a weekly radio programme, and CDs of both contemporary and traditional music. Local fieldworkers have been trained to take photographs, make films and sound recordings in their home communities. The museum has also created a very particular context for the return of visual and audio materials.

Research project in Malakula. © Haidy Geismar

In addition to the development of strong relationships with museums and archives that facilitate an ongoing stream of images from overseas returning to the National Museum's archive, the National Cultural Research Policy, signed by all visiting researchers, stipulates that a copy of every image and recording made by visiting researchers must be deposited in the museum as well as given to the people with whom they were made. As such, an ethos of return is built into every international collaboration, and nearly every research project, no matter what its subject, will bring more images and recordings into circulation within this framework.

I have likened the process of working with these photographs to a form of archaeology—we used the photographs to dig down, beneath the overgrown bush and the coconut trees, to the layer beneath, made visible on the paper images for the first time in many years. Atchin and Vao men were eager to retrace Layard's images onto the contemporary contours of the island. Complementing the archival research of Anita Herle, in Cambridge, my research was increasingly configured around the process of re-photographing Layard's images, held up by the people of that place, where they were originally taken. Digging down with images, we uncovered, amongst other things, one of the last standing slit-drums on the island, at Amal Tara, Senhar. >

Walking across the islands with Layard's photographs and the process of re-photography this initiated had to be negotiated in each place that we visited—on occasion we were not allowed to photograph a site because the person who 'owned' the place, from whom we needed permission, was not present. We also encountered several disputes about who had the right to have their photograph taken in particular places. In one visit to a dancing-ground on Vao we photographed an elder who had not been present during our first visit. He had been angered not because of any prior connection that he held to Layard but because he was the most authoritative person in that area, and should have had his photograph taken first as a matter of protocol. This highlights how photographic practice is always negotiated between the photographer and the photographed, and that the movement of photographic images is also a negotiable activity. Taking images back into communities is about layering information within a contemporary political landscape, moving from 'archive' to 'living entity'.[6] It also shows us how the reproducible nature of photographic technology, in this case the photocopying and re-photographing of Layard's images, has the power to respond to local meanings.

Walking around Atchin and Vao with Layard's images taught me how both taking and looking at photographs is an embodied practice, deeply embedded within local experience, and started to highlight how ideas about evidence are matched with ideas about malleability in assigning meanings and memories to images. In matching Layard's photographs to their contemporary referents, I became aware that many of the images embody Layard's own pathways across these small islands. Most particularly, Layard's panoramic views of the dancing grounds encapsulate a sense of being immersed in the cultural geography of the islands and highlight how being embedded in this landscape played an important role in building Layard's understanding of ritual practice on Vao and Atchin.

The images themselves impart a sense of 'being' in particular places on Vao and Atchin, a sense strong enough to inspire similarly evocative activities. The people I worked with not only matched the contemporary environment of the islands to Layard's images, they used their own bodies to form connections between the two. Men on Atchin and Vao stage managed the process of re-photography by positioning themselves within the frame of the new images we were creating, touching a drum or tree they recognised from the photograph and as a part of their own personal heritage. These acts of re-photography and re-enactment of the past were both mimetic and creative. Layard's images were consolidated as embodiments of connections between places, people and their ancestors, and the taking of a new set of photographs became an important articulation of these people's connection to their ancestral land, and of the contemporary tracing of these histories.

In the first photograph (on p. 181) you can see Abison Meltekaon from Or Tamat and Marcel Pierre from Emil Lep, standing at the site of Layard's photograph (see opposite), holding up the photocopy of the original image, which they are mimicking in their own stance. The fact of this new photograph—that it was essentially commissioned to show something very specific (the connection of a group of people to a particular place)—alters how we may perceive the original image. It was very likely that Layard's photographs were produced with a similar intention—that, even then, people were using the process of photography (in an environment where they had no access to cameras, and very little access to photographic negatives or prints) to stake similar claims. By staking such a claim, in a medium and format that has less resonance locally, it also seems as though the people in Layard's original photograph were well aware of the power of photographic images to circulate, and wanted their image to circulate as broadly as possible. This is conjecture, of course, but seeing the ways in which photographs are embedded in social relations, and witnessing how the practice of photography, along with that of making and embedding images in wider systems of knowledge and interpretation, highlights the intrinsically collaborative nature of the medium.

John Layard, Malakula, 1914–15.
© University of Cambridge Museum
of Archeology and Anthropology

1   Chris Pinney, 'The parallel histories of
    anthropology and photography', in
    Elizabeth Edwards (ed.), *Anthropology
    and Photography 1860–1920* (New Haven,
    CT: Yale University Press, 1992), pp. 74–95.
    Anita Herle and Sandra Rouse (eds),
    *Cambridge and the Torres Strait: Centena-
    ry Essays on the 1898 Anthropological
    Expedition* (Cambridge: Cambridge Uni-
    versity Press, 1998). Especially Chapter 1,
    'Introduction' and Chapter 5 by Elizabeth
    Edwards, 'Performing science: still
    photography and the Torres Strait Expedition'.

    Anita Herle, Jude Philp and Leilani
    Bin Juda, 'The journey of the stars: Gab
    Titui a cultural centre for the Torres Strait',
    in Nick Stanley (ed.), *The Future of Indigenous
    Museums* (Oxford: Berg, 2007), pp. 93–116.
2   The project is funded by the Australian
    Research Council and led by Jane Lydon at
    the University of Western Australia.
3   James Clifford, *Routes: Travel and Transla-
    tion in the Late Twentieth Century* (Cambridge,
    MA: Harvard University Press, 1997).
4   Clare Harris and Michael O'Hanlon,
    'The future of the ethnographic museum',

    Anthropology Today (2013), vol. 29, No. 1, pp. 8–12.
5   Haidy Geismar and Anita Herle, *Moving
    Images: John Layard, fieldwork and
    Photography on Malakula since 1914*
    (Honolulu, HI: Hawaii University Press,
    2010).
6   Elizabeth Edwards, 'Negotiating spaces:
    some photographic incidents in the
    Western Pacific, 1883–84', in Joan
    Schwartz and James Ryan (eds), *Picturing
    Place: Photography and the Geographical
    Imagination* (London: Tauris, 2003),
    pp. 261–280.

Foto

THOMAS BALL
MURRAY BALLARD
SAM FAULKNER
SOPHIE GERRARD
JONATHAN GOLDBERG
AMANDA JACKSON
JASON LARKIN
VALENTINA QUINTANO
SYD SHELTON
NICK WAPLINGTON

Document

Certain images are hard to shake.

Pictures can pinpoint moments of collective history and of personal significance. They can embody the very best and worst of our communities, and our world.

I'm sure many of us can picture still the photograph of the lone student protestor who, in June 1989, stood defiant before a procession of tanks to halt their progress into Beijing's Tiananmen Square.

There's a wonderful image, of personal significance to me, that I can picture still with crystal clarity. It was a photograph of a woman named Petra Kelly, who co-founded the German Green Party, and who has been the greatest inspiration of my political life. The image showed her, on her first day as a German MP, entering Parliament with armfuls of sunflowers and wearing jeans. The image conveyed so much all at once: a rich joy and sense of hope, and Petra's demonstration of politics as something personal—that everything we do is political, from when we get up in the morning to what we buy, eat and wear.

Some images—and the arts more broadly—can make us uncomfortable. They can challenge, even compel us, to reassess our priorities and question our realities. They can transcend barriers as they spark local debate and inspire global change.

It is imperative that we identify and utilise the tools that best communicate our messages. The visual arts are crucial in this regard, and we would do well not to underestimate their potential for raising social, political and environmental awareness and provoking urgent debates.

Although we now know a lot about climate change, we don't yet know enough about what influences people to change their behaviours. This is one of the reasons I'm excited to welcome the One Planet Living photo-narrative project to our city this year, which will be installed for Brighton Photo Biennial. Showcasing positive environmental messages, projects like this can reach sections of the population who will respond to its powerful imagery.

One Planet Living sums itself up neatly on its website. If everyone lived like the average European, it points out, we'd need three planets to live on. That number rises to five if we're talking about the USA—five planet Earths. That's really where One Planet Living begins. It seeks to help people live well, using less.

Based around ten sustainability principles, the initiative outlines how the Earth's resources can accommodate all of its inhabitants perfectly well, if only we'd share them out more fairly. The principles cover everything from zero-waste and carbon communities to sustainable transport and water, local produce and economies, land use, culture and communities.

The One Planet Living photography project brings together ten talented photographers—from right here in Brighton as well as from around the world—to visually document each of the ten One Planet Living principles. The works will be installed according to theme in ten key public spaces across our city.

Last year we became the first One Planet Living City in the world. Brighton and Hove is fantastically creative and so receptive to conversations around these issues. That we should host this photography project is brilliantly apt, and I'm excited to see it take root.

The images will remain *in situ* for ten months, and I urge everyone to take the time to appreciate them in full, to see what impact they have upon you.

I know—from experience—that a lone voice in Parliament can make a difference. I also know that the more voices backing me, the greater the impetus for change. Every voice counts, and standing up and making ours heard matters. It makes a difference.

But that awareness and support and debate has to take root somewhere. And it might just start with an image that is hard to shake.

Sophie Gerrard

Pineapple, community composting, Brighton, 2014

Murry Ballard

Charcoal burning, Saddlescombe Farm, 2014

Amanda Jackson

Daisy with her creations at the Toy Hacking Workshop run
by Exploring Senses, 2014

Jason Larkin

Essex Place. Apartment buildings being retrofitted with new outer wall insulation to improve their energy efficiency, 2014

Sam Faulkner

Chicken roaming through the orchard, Orchard Eggs

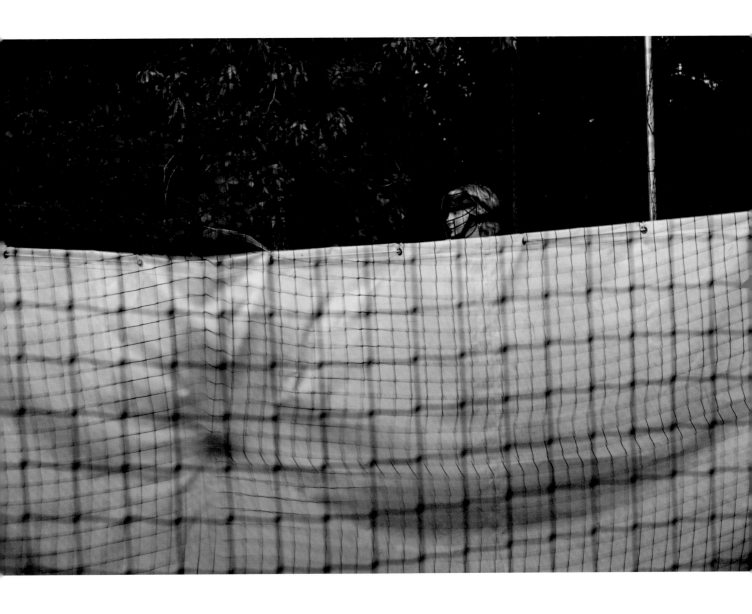

Valentina Quintano

Henfield Women's Cricket Club, training session

Jonathan Goldberg

Affectionate embracing, 2014

Syd Shelton

Nick Waplington

Economy II, public toilet, South Downs National Park, 2014

Thomas Ball

Peacehaven Wastewater Treatment Works, 2014

The Body Allotropic: Photography and Sculpture

Above: Andrew Lacon, *Studio Collage (Bernini)*, 2014
Right: Andrew Lacon, Work in Progress, Steel, curtain, 2014

Jonathan P. Watts

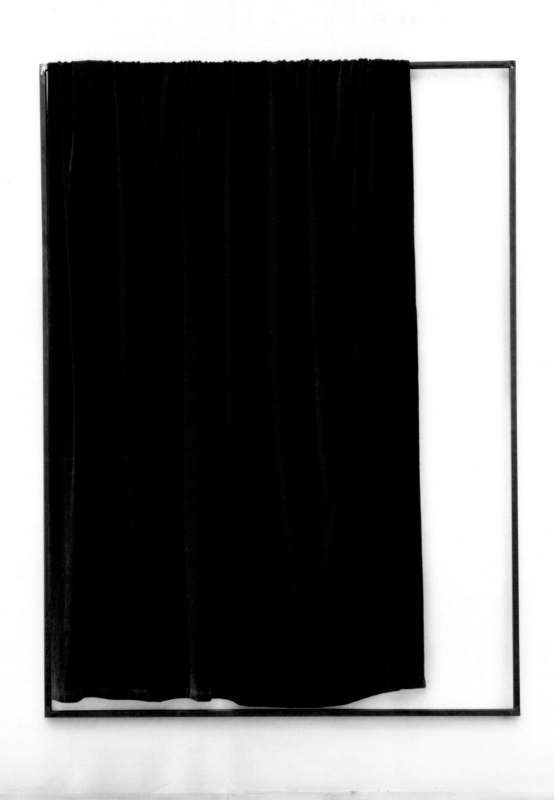

Artists Andrew Lacon and Cornford & Cross share a long-standing interest in relationships between photography and sculpture. Writer Jonathan Watts explores the sometimes complex ways in which the different media interact and illuminate each other.

I will begin with drowning. Two water-logged bodies, pulled in 171 years apart, affirm photography's identity as both document and art. The many relays and returns between these two drowned men, martyrs for the cause, dramatise the complex relations between photography and sculpture. The first stinking body is that of Hippolyte Bayard, re-presented in his direct positive photographic print titled *La Noyé (Self-portrait as a Drowned Man)*, taken on 18 October 1840; the second is Jeremy Millar's *Self-portrait as a Drowned Man (The Willows)*, a mimetic silicon and fibreglass model of the artist, adorned in his hair and clothes, as a drowned man, produced in 2011.

Bayard produced three points of view of himself as a man driven to suicide by despair after the French Académie des Sciences vetoed his contribution to the invention of photography. These posed, serial photographs depict 'H.B.' propped stiffly upright, wrapped in drapery, surrounded by a ceramic vase, large straw hat and a small plaster statuette of a crouching nymph. Bayard owned around 40 such statuettes, and made numerous photographs of them in careful arrangements, frequently including himself in the frame.[1] In one of these, he communes with miniature putti and Roman scholars set in relief; another shows a Sophoclean head, curlicued hair and beard, levitating, disembodied, at his shoulder.

Within the photographic frame, Bayard and his statuettes co-mingle, reduced to two-dimensionality; the result is a general equivalence in which we witness fantastical exchanges between animate and inanimate things (if it were not such a long exposure I would say they 'cavort'). Should we not already be convinced of Bayard's statuesquery, we learn from a text on the reverse of *La Noyé* that he is pictured having already occupied the mortuary for three days—more than adequate time for his rigor mortis limbs to ossify into stone-like columns.

Jeremy Millar, *Self-portrait as a Drowned Man (The Willows)*, 2011

Unlike the ontologically flat photographic print, Millar's mimetic, volumetric body occupies human dimensions. It takes seriously Bayard's photo-generated fantasy of becoming an object. It is, I would argue, a photograph by other means, an extension into three dimensions that confounds the flat, rectangular expectations of photography. It bodies forth what Steve Edwards has called, borrowing a term from chemistry, the 'allotropic' nature of photography: like carbon, it can be useful but ugly coal *and* useless yet beautiful diamond—both document (a mechanical copy of nature) and picture (an artistic representation).

In 1851, Bayard, along with Édouard Baldus, was the first photographer employed by the Mission Héliographique, a photographic survey established by order of the Commission des monuments, to travel through the French regions documenting historical monuments. Several years later, in 1855, the Reverend F. A. S. Marshall lectured to an audience on the necessity of a similar photographic survey of major sculptural

Hippolyte Bayard, *La Noyé*
(*Self-portrait as a Drowned Man*), 1840

Cornford & Cross, *Why Read the Classics*, 2005.
Film lamp and reflector on marble statue, Rome, Italy

and architectural works in England. Marshall presented
a photograph taken at Notre Dame, Paris: 'Look',
he implored, 'at the rich mass of Sculpture over the West
Door ... What more could you desire to bring before you
than the work and genius of the Sculptor? What could
be more truthful than this, the very impress of the object?'[2]

Beginning with Henry Fox Talbot's *The Pencil of
Nature* (1844–46)—the first photobook—the reproduction
of works of art was regarded as one of photography's
primary spheres of activity: besides architectural details,
it contained two photographic illustrations of a bust of
Patroclus. 'Statues, busts, and other specimens of sculpture', Fox Talbot wrote, 'are generally well represented
by the Photographic Art; and also very rapidly, in consequence of their whiteness.'[3] And, unlike living men and
women, for whom there were contraptions to arrest their
bodies for long exposures, statues and plaster casts
were patient, ever-willing subjects for the photographer.
Elsewhere in *The Pencil of Nature*, Fox Talbot also
observes that 'a very great number of different effects
may be obtained from [photographing] a single speci-
men of sculpture'.

Around the infancy of photography then, between
Bayard, Fox Talbot and the lesser-known Marshall,
we can deduce judgements on how sculpture should
be photographed. Is it expressive, with the propensity
for a 'very great number of effects'? Or does it guarantee,
immutably the 'very impress of the object'? Can it not
be both? A further question is posed about the location
of value: is it with the assumed-present object or the artfulness of the photograph that mediates? >

Cornford & Cross, *Afterimage I*, 2012. Aluminium substrate
after removal and destruction of artists' photograph

Throughout the 19th century, and into the 20th, numerous photographic surveys of sculpture were carried out. Key among them are Arthur Kingsley Porter's *Romanesque Sculpture of the Pilgrimage Roads* (1923), Adolph Braun's museological photography, Clarence Kennedy's multi-volume *Studies in the History and Criticism of Sculpture* (1928–32), and the archaeologist Esther B. van Deman's photographs of Rome. In 1881, Albrecht Meydenbauer, Director of the Royal Prussian Photogrammetric Institution, initiated his survey to establish an archive of monuments. Meydenbauer's intention was to include photographs on the basis of which a building could be reconstructed photogrammetrically—utilising the mathematical quantifiable measure of central perspective—in all the details of its ground and vertical plans 100 years after it had disappeared from the Earth.[4]

Anticipating, willing even, the disappearance of the object, Sir Oliver Wendell Holmes wrote in his 1859 essay 'The stereoscope and the stereograph':

Form is henceforth divorced from matter. In fact, matter as a visible object is of no great use any longer, except as the mould on which form is shaped. Give us a few negatives of a thing worth seeing, taken from different points of view, and that is all we want of it. Pull it down or burn it up, if you please.[5]

This enthused orphaning of artefacts—a strange blend of idolatry and iconoloclasm—anticipates the recuperative guardianship of André Malraux's 'Musée imaginaire', first described by the French Minister of Cultural Affairs in 1947. Like Walter Benjamin in his 'Work of art' essay, Malraux identified the initial decontextualisation of artefacts in the 19th century with the invention of the museum—a storehouse for amassing and viewing things ripped from their sites of origin, 'cut loose from all referentiality to the use, representational or ritual, for which they might have been created'. Reproduced in art books, postcards and posters, these works were doubly decontextualised: unmoored, circulating far beyond their original context, tradition shattered, aura liquidated.

For Malraux, this liquidated aura, engendered by mechanical reproduction, is what 'allows all of the fragments to course together in the River of History, of what he calls "the persisting life of certain forms, emerging ever and again like spectres from the past"'.[6] Malraux envisioned a global, universalised art history, not so dissimilar to the ethic of Edward Steichen's *Family of Man* exhibition (1955), an archive that could redistribute attention to the previously overlooked. The history of art, Malraux asserted, had become 'the history of that which can be photographed'. (Isn't our age of digital museums without walls mirrored by the digital archive without museums?) >

Cornford & Cross, *A Month in the Country*, 2003.
Rights-managed commercial stock photographs
hired for one month, then whitewashed over

To what extent was this redistribution of attention keyed into visual pleasure? 'If the work of sculpture', Mary Bergstein writes, 'is to be considered the primary referent, then the intervening photographic process, with its inevitable subjectivity, propels the representational image away from the referent, if psychologically closer to the beholder.'[7] Bergstein has insisted that the documentary field of sculpture warrants its own special area of art historiography; it is a history unto itself. In fact, at the turn of the 19th century, the German art historian Heinrich Wölfflin did advocate formulaic approaches to the reproduction of art works for scholarly purposes. In *How One Should Photograph Sculpture* he suggests that lighting could be determined by looking at paintings and drawings from the same period of the statue or relief being photographed. Similarly, the point of view should correspond to the original intention of the sculptor.[8]

Unless taken serially (as in *La Noyé*), photography assumes a mono-focal point of view in relation to a static thing. A moving image shot with a mobile camera seems to deliver movement to stillness, approximating our own movement of bodies in space, and poly-focal points of view. Consider, for example, Rossellini's *Journey to Italy* (1954), Henri Alekan's *L'Enfer de Rodin* (1957), Straub-Huillet's *A Visit to the Louvre* (2004) or, more recently, Lucy Skaer and Rosalind Nashashibi's *Flash in the Metropolitan* (2006). Each constructs complex identifications, captured by narrative, with the camera. But in each are we not still locked into a monocular point of view?

In the late 1960s, Jan Dibbets's *Perspective Correction* photographs (1968) and David Hall's moving image work *VERTICAL* (1969) signalled a permanent shift in the experience of space and sculpture. Both demonstrate how point of view, mediated by the camera, can actually be constitutive of sculpture, while commenting on the radical dislocation of the actual experience of space and its representation on a two-dimensional surface. To parrot the critic Craig Owens on Robert Smithson, here the notion of point of view is no longer a function of physical position but of the mode (photographic, cinematic, textual) of confrontation with the work of art.

Into the 1960s it was recognised that photographers could identify and represent the sculptural quality of configurations in the world: think, for example, of Man Ray's photographs of objects such as a typewriter, Walker Evans's clapboard shacks or the Bechers' water towers. Absent here is the production of 'work' *as such* existing before and outside the photographic—'the absence of anything with the status of sculpture beyond its existence in and as a photograph'.[9] There is a relation to Duchamp's ready-mades—he referred to them as his *instantanés* (snapshots)—which translate into the third dimension the same photographic principle of selection and representation. Duchamp intended the readymade to exist independently of the artist as a negation of the expressive, authorial gesture of the painter. These were largely reasons why in the 1960s the impersonal photograph became a prime tool for the documentation of expanded concepts of sculpture. Here, we can think about John Stezaker's *Works 1969-1971*, Sigmar Polke's *Bamboo Pole Loves Folding Ruler Star* (1968–69) or Smithson's *A Tour of the Monuments of Passaic, New Jersey* (1967). The only thing guaranteeing the event's endurance is the photograph itself.

As early as 1969, Peter Bunnell, who would go on to organise the seminal exhibition *Photography into Sculpture* at the Museum of Modern Art, New York, in 1970, called attention to the 'photographic artefact' considered as sculpture in itself. The following year, 23 artists showed in *Photography into Sculpture*, each exploring the photograph as a physical object, many bleeding the medium into other media that had traditionally been kept separate. Robert Heinecken's *Multiple Solution Puzzle* (1965), for example, collected 16 black and white tile-like photographs on a wooden base; Robert Watts's *BLT* (1965) embeds cut-ups of black-and-white photo transparency into a transparent acylic block; and Jerry McMillan's *Torn Bag* (1968) displays a lunch sack ripped open to reveal a landscape view. >

Cornford & Cross, *Reference Works No. 12*, 2013. Painted steel

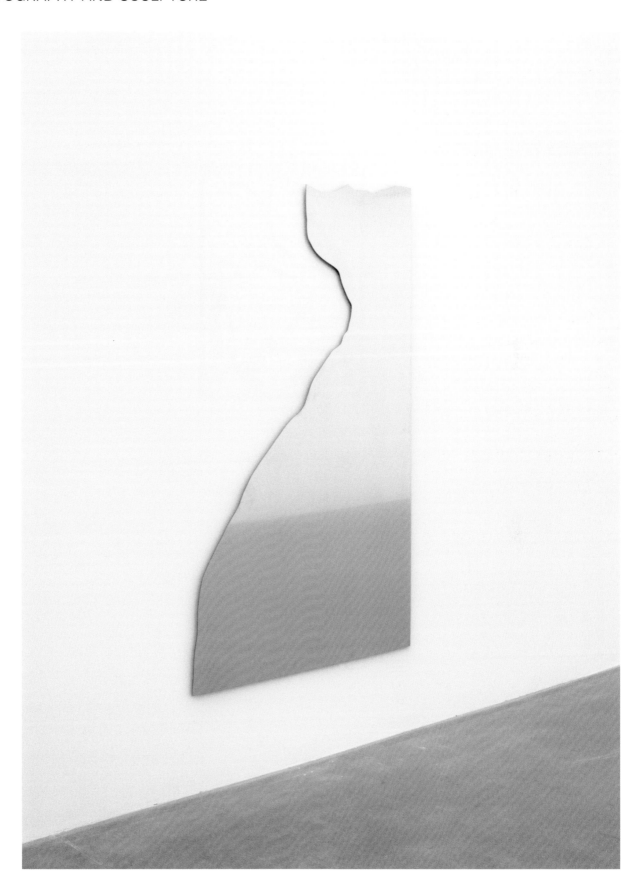

Cornford & Cross, *Agalmatophilia: Fig. 1*, 2013. Painted aluminium

Andrew Lacon, *Reproduction*, 2014. A4 Photocopy (297 × 210 mm)

Cornford & Cross *The White Bear Effect*, 2013
LED screen showing Olympic highlights (4 × 3 m)
De La Warr Pavilion, Bexhill, East Sussex

In Roland Barthes' beguiling narrative of photography, *Camera Lucida*, the flatness of the photograph is a surface he can only sweep over: 'I cannot penetrate, cannot reach into the Photograph. I can only sweep it with my glance, like a smooth surface. The Photograph is *flat*, platitudinous in the true sense of the word.' Yet, the volumetric expansion of photography in space forces us to look at photography rather than through it—it grates our vision, becomes haptic. Two years ago, the Los Angeles-based gallery Cherry & Martin restaged a version of Bunnell's exhibition, receiving critical praise from the art press at a moment when many shows of that period seemed to be dumbly restaged. The exhibition of photography in three-dimensional space looked remarkably prescient, particularly today when many contemporary photographers are using expanded notions of photography to re-examine the medium and its relationship to sculpture.

Sara VanDerBeek's photographs of blue-painted busts of Roman women return a look that long pre-dates the age of mechanical reproduction; Taiyo Onorato and Nico Krebs's whimsical turtle and armadillo cameras transform the architecture of the photographic apparatus into sculptural artefacts; Giuseppe Gabellone constructs a chaotic roller-coaster structure in miniature, takes the photograph, then disassembles it; Andrew Lacon makes the historiography of photography of Roman sculpture

a subject of photographic scrutiny; Oliver Laric (like Wendell Holmes before him) collaborates experimentally with the Lincoln Collection to produce three-dimensional scans of their artefacts; in Lorenzo Vitturi's *Dalston Anatomy* (2013), the rich texture of his photographic surfaces dissolve into the texture of his sculptural assemblage; motifs migrate from Becky Beasley's photographic images into ceramic matter, and back again; Cornford & Cross have, among other things, painted out framed photographs; and Mark Leckey, Liz Deschene and Hito Steyerl each, in their own way, use chromakey green screens as backdrops with the propensity to make sculpture or context disappear.

The relations between photography and sculpture are richly multifaceted, dating back to the former's earliest days when a man drowned to make a monument to its 'allotropic' status as both document and picture. The second drowned man is a monument to photography by other means, not narrowly defined.

1   Geoffrey Batchen, *Burning With Desire* (Cambridge, MA: MIT Press, 1999), p. 162.

2   Geraldine A. Johnson, 'The very impress of the object: photographing sculpture from Fox Talbot to the present day', in Geraldine A. Johnson (ed.), *Sculpture and Photography: Envisioning the Third Dimension* (Cambridge: Cambridge University Press, 1999), p. 1.

3   William H. Fox Talbot, *The Pencil of Nature*, part 1 (London: Longman, Brown, Green and Longmans, 1844), plate V.

4   Jens Schröter, 'Archive—post/ photographic', http://www. medienkunstnetz.de/themes/photo_byte/ archive_post_photographic (17 June 2014).

5   Sir Oliver Wendell Holmes, 'The stereoscope and the stereograph', in Alan Trachtenberg (ed.), *Classic Essays on Photography* (New York: Leete's Island Books, 1980), p. 80.

6   Hal Foster, 'Archives of modern art', in *Design and Crime (And Other Diatribes)*

(Cambridge, MA: MIT Press, 2011), p. 79.

7   Mary Bergstein, 'Lonely Aphrodites: on the documentary photography of sculpture', *Art Bulletin* (1992), vol. 74, No. 3, p. 475.

8   Geraldine A. Johnson, op. cit., p. 9.

9   Tobia Bezzola, 'From sculpture in photography to photography as plastic art', in Geoffrey Batchen, Tobia Bezzola and Roxana Marcoci (eds), *The Original Copy: Photography of Sculpture, 1839 to Today* (New York: The Museum of Modern Art, 2010), p. 30.

The Amazing Analogue

JAN VON HOLLEBEN

in Conversation with

AARON SCHUMAN

All images © Jan von Holleben from *The Amazing Analogue: How we play photography* commission for Hove Museum and Brighton Photo Biennial 2014

Aaron Schuman: To start, you're very fond of a quote by Mark Twain (which appears on the homepage of your website and in your email signature): 'What work I have done I have done because it has been play. If it had been work I shouldn't have done it.' Could you explain the relevance of this quote—and of 'play' itself—to both your artistic practice and your general philosophy towards it?

Jan von Holleben: The core of play theory and the *homo ludens*—'the man who plays'—is that one learns and understands both oneself and the world through play. Play is the most natural way of learning. In a game, players move, act and decide on what to do in a pseudo-real environment, where one can test things out without fear of genuinely losing. This advances personal skills, confidence and knowledge on various levels, be it social, political, technical, economic or otherwise. Sometimes I manage to find adults who are keen, brave or simply still able to play properly, but it's for this reason that I often work with children—they're good players, and do it automatically until they are told to stop, and are encouraged to adhere to social boundaries when they are at an age that is considered 'grown up'. Sadly this is a very Western and somewhat contemporary phenomenon. But many cultures still engage in play through games, dance, theatre, festivals, group activities and so on. The Olympic Games originate from this—cultural understanding through play—and, as the World Cup demonstrates, these traditions of learning and understanding one another through play still continue somewhat, even in the West.

I see myself as part of a larger society, and I understand that cultural and social development can be strongly supported by creativity and freedom—both of which define playing. Whenever I make work, for either myself or others (in terms of commissions and so on), I always start the process with a question or a brief, which needs to be answered by the end of the project. Sometimes this can be very philosophical, such as 'How will society change in the future?' Sometimes it's straightforward, such as 'How can you visually represent the relationship between two people?' or 'How can you illustrate a particular song or a story?' Then I treat the project as if it were a game.

My starting point is always a visual archive—either the one I've collected in my own memory or one already out in the world—which I begin to edit down. In a sense, I see this as my 'playground' for the project. Then I begin to think about some basic features that I'd like to include as part of the project—props, people, locations and so on—as well as the specific time and place where the resulting images will appear or exist in the world. If this game requires extra players—such as models, actors, friends, other artists or whomever—then I invite them to join in the game as well. All of these things define the rules of the game. As soon as I have gathered all of this, I start to sketch out my ideas.

When the photo-shoot finally happens, everything is in place and everyone who is taking part knows the rules of the game. This is when the game actually starts, and when the images themselves actually begin to develop. By the nature of my games, we usually have plenty of fun and also a lot of freedom in terms of the outcome. In my visual world, and in the techniques that I use in my work, everything is possible—we can fly to a distant universe, build machines that can otherwise only be dreamt of, see ghosts, or shrink ourselves to dwarf-size; there are no limits apart from our own responsibilities and skills. This is when my work becomes a collaborative group effort; the more input, creativity and effort each player puts into the game, the more exciting it gets. This is how we play photography.

So, as Mark Twain describes it, I see my work as play. I know that I produce my best work when I approach it as if I'm playing a game, rather than constructing a classically structured work environment that is led by authoritative means. >

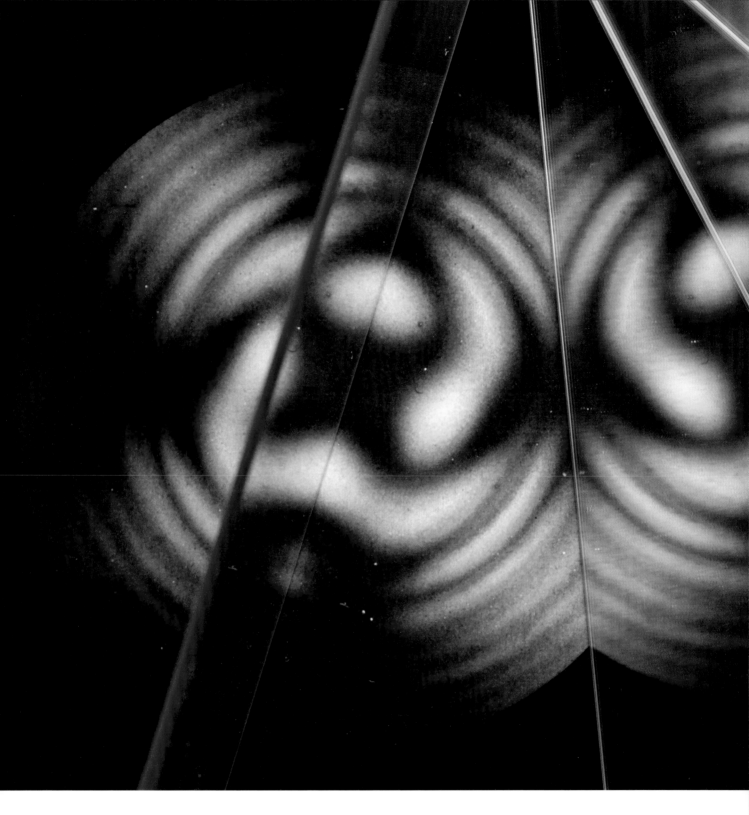

AS: How did your Brighton Photo Biennial 2014 commission come about?

JVH: I was commissioned by the Brighton Photo Biennial to look at, and be inspired by, a wonderful archive of images and material held within the Hove Museum & Art Gallery's collection, which was made by pioneering filmmakers about a century ago. Around that time, films, projections and magic lantern shows were just beginning to be publicly exhibited, and were very much in their early stages, so there was a lot of experimentation going on, and visual trickery was at a peak. Things such as colour film and narrative visual language were being tested and presented to various audiences for the first time, often in theatrical and magical environments. George Albert Smith (1864–1959), who's one of the main people that I'm focusing upon, was a trickster, inventor and illusionist. Before getting involved with film, he was a performer, and he often used aspects of early photography within his performances; then he began giving magic lantern shows that involved a series of 'dissolving views', in which he skilfully manipulated the lantern's lenses to show changes in time, perspective and location, which helped him to tell stories. So he—and many of the other Hove-based film pioneers represented in the Hove Museum's collection—were utilising state-of-the-art technology and skills in photography, projection, filmmaking and analogue techniques—such as sequencing, vignetting, double-exposure and special lenses—to produce spectacular shows for audiences that had never seen things like edited moving images, narrative film or basic special effects.

Today, 100 years later, digital imagery is doing the same thing again. But if you look at my work over the last decade or so, you'll notice that I generally play with a digitally native audience by introducing non-digital image solutions. I think that it's because of this aspect of my work, as well as the importance of play and collaboration in my creative process, that the BPB14 curatorial board approached me with this particular commission. They asked me if I'd be interested in exploring the museum's collection, and producing a collaborative project that involved local children.

AS: Tell me about the title of your project— *The Amazing Analogue*?

JVH: On first sight, people generally assume that my images are produced digitally, because that is the norm today, and they don't expect anything different from me. But as soon as they discover a clue that reveals a problem within their reading of my images, and their digital assumptions, they are often amazed that the analogue can do such things. So in one sense, this project relates to the analogue techniques used by Smith and others, and contextualises them both historically and contemporarily. But on the other hand, I am recontextualising these processes within today's digital culture, applying purely analogue techniques to my own work, and creating an 'amazing analogue' moment for an audience that is used to digital image manipulation. It is a little revolution for 'the amazing analogue'.

AS: In this project, you're working with a number of young people from the Brighton and Hove community, with whom you are exploring and then interpreting this rather mysterious archive of images. First, tell me about the archive itself; and, secondly, how are you introducing the young people to the images, and guiding them to engage with and interpret them?

JVH: When I first visited the Hove Museum, I discovered the archive I mentioned earlier—a set of boxes that had been donated to the museum by an old man several years ago, which included hundreds of photographic slides and negatives that had made for The Kromscop, one of the first RGB projectors. The images themselves came from filmmakers, photographers, performers and projectionists, many of whom were actually from Hove. This particular collection of images grabbed my interest specifically because they had no obvious connections amongst them. They show a huge variety of subjects such as portraits, interiors, photographs of sculptures and diagrams—but mostly they are abstract images, and therefore we don't actually know what was photographed; they lie entirely outside our own knowledge and understanding. Surely some of them were taken with special microscopic devices (we actually found images of such apparatuses), and others must have been taken with special lenses, which make them look rather psychedelic, but we don't know what they are. But it's also apparent that the photographers who made them weren't amateurs, as the pictures clearly contain many aspects of professionalism. >

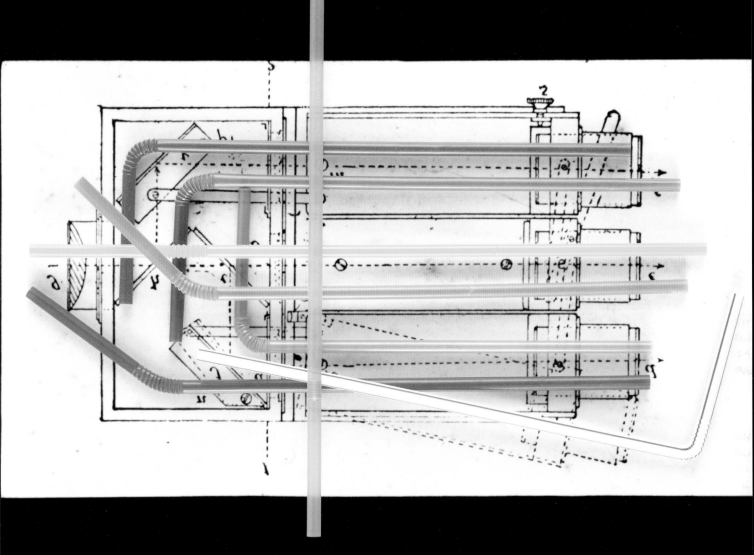

So, as a photographer I asked myself: 'For what purpose were these images taken?', 'What is this collection all about?' and, even more interestingly, 'What do we see in these images?' As a collection they do not make sense, but instead contain a kind of magical atmosphere. So, the images that I found in those boxes just kept me thinking and wondering.

Then I began working with a team of children, all of whom are young carers between eight and 12 years old, who live in Brighton and Hove. When I met the kids for the first time I selected about 30 images to show them, in order to sensitise them to the project, and we decided to edit all of the images down and somehow try to bring sense to them. We discussed what these images could possibly depict, why they might have been taken, how they might have been taken, and dug further into the archive in order to find similar images, as well as other traces and clues that might help us to answer some of these questions, such as images of photographic studios and equipment.

Eventually, we decided that many of our questions could only be answered by specially built machines, which could interpret the images for us. So, I proposed that we actually build these machines—just as the early photographers did to interpret their reality—and customise them to decipher these particular images for us. I suggested we might be able to find answers by playing the same games that the original photographers played. So, I asked the children to sketch machines, and talk about what features their machine would need in order to process the images. Most telling so far is the 'Machine for Hypnotic Images': the images are inserted into it, and go through a number of stages before a very particular light source—similar to a dentist's light—flickers into a 'patient's'/viewer's eyes in order to hypnotise them, and make them understand what the image is all about. But obviously much of this is top secret—as it is with all magical super machines—so we cannot tell you too much about them, apart from that they work flawlessly!

AS: How has this very collaborative project involved your own creative approach and experience?

JVH: The collaborative process of making this project is artistic and playful, rather than scientific or logical. As I see it, science and common logic can harm the creative and playful process very easily sometimes, and my work usually deals with the impossibility of reality anyway. I'm always interested in jumping between imagination, vision and reality—blurring their borders and including the audience in the process. Furthermore, along with having an artistic practice that relies upon playing and learning, professionally I have also become somewhat of a problem-solver, finding visual solutions for commercial briefs that are not meant to be answered with 'straight' photography. And additionally, my initial training—as a teacher for disabled children—and my general interest in child education are very much a part of the collaborative aspect of this project. Usually I only need to use a few of my skills at a time, but this project has demanded that I use many skills simultaneously, so it's been full speed on all channels, and, in the process of creating *The Amazing Analogue*, many aspects of my life and work have come full circle.

Honestly, I'm just so proud of what we've done: both the process and its results are so exciting, and I know that the whole experience has been incredibly productive and engaging—for me personally, as well as for the kids, the museum's curators and the institution itself. And considering the biennial's theme, collaboration has certainly been the most vital and rewarding part of this project.

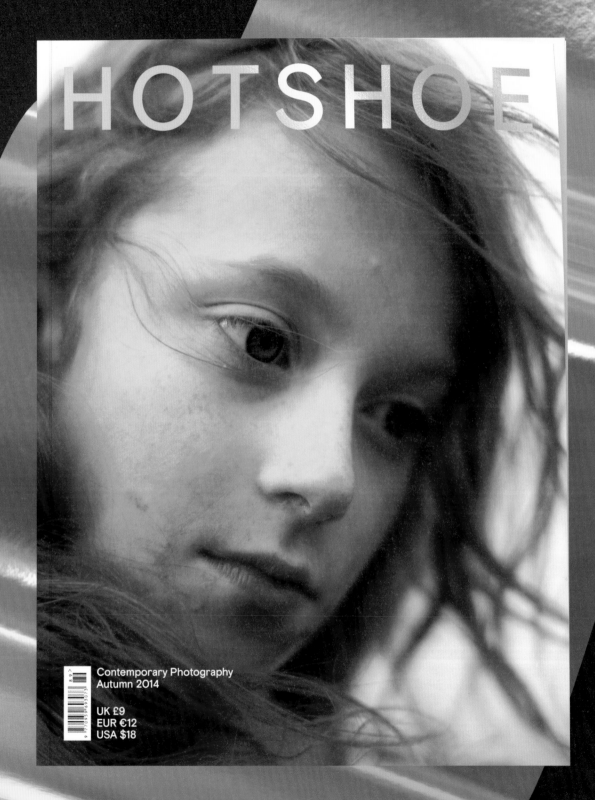

Contemporary Photography

HOTSHOE

Contemporary Photography
Autumn 2014

UK £9
EUR €12
USA $18

hotshoemagazine.com

Concrete print, from the series 'Landscapes of Uncertainty' © Jim Woodall, printed using our Direct to Media printing service.

Collaboration, Innovation, Dedication, Emotion.

We believe this is what makes great work, outstanding.

And that's why our premier Photographic Printing, Mounting and Framing services include all of the above.

JERWOOD
PHOTOWORKS
AWARDS
2015

CALL FOR ENTRIES

The inaugural Jerwood/Photoworks Awards seek outstanding proposals in relation to new approaches to photography.

Three Awards of £5,000 to support the making of new work, a mentoring programme, access to a production fund and group exhibition at Jerwood Space, London.

Closing Date:
5pm 1 December 2014

For full details and selectors visit
www.photoworks.org.uk/JPA15
#JPA15

JERWOOD **CHARITABLE FOUNDATION**   **photoworks**    Supported by **ARTS COUNCIL ENGLAND**

The Edmond J. Safra Fountain Court © Marcus Ginns

PHOTO
LONDON

"NEW YORK WAS
THE CENTRE OF
THE ART WORLD.
NOW IT'S LONDON."

–YOKO ONO

Photo London,

Somerset House 21-24 May 2015.

Now open for gallery applications.

www.photolondon.org

Martin Parr
Black Country Stories

The New Art Gallery Walsall
Gallery Square
Walsall WS2 8LG

thenewartgallerywalsall.org.uk

4 October, 2014 to
11 January, 2015

Over the last 4 years,
Magnum photographer,
Martin Parr, has created a
photographic portrait and
archive of life in the Black
Country through photography,
film and oral histories.

Commissioned by Multistory,
working in partnership with
The New Art Gallery Walsall and
Wolverhampton Art Gallery.

Norman Soper (best pot leek),
Sandwell Show, 2010
© Martin Parr / Magnum Photos

PARIS PHOTO

13.16 NOV 2014
GRAND PALAIS

21—25 January 2015
Business Design Centre
Islington, London N1

londonartfair.co.uk

Photography Focus Day
21 January 2015
Photo50 curated by Sheyi Bankale

MODERN BRITISH AND CONTEMPORARY ART

ART PROJECTS | PHOTO 50 | LON DON ART FAIR

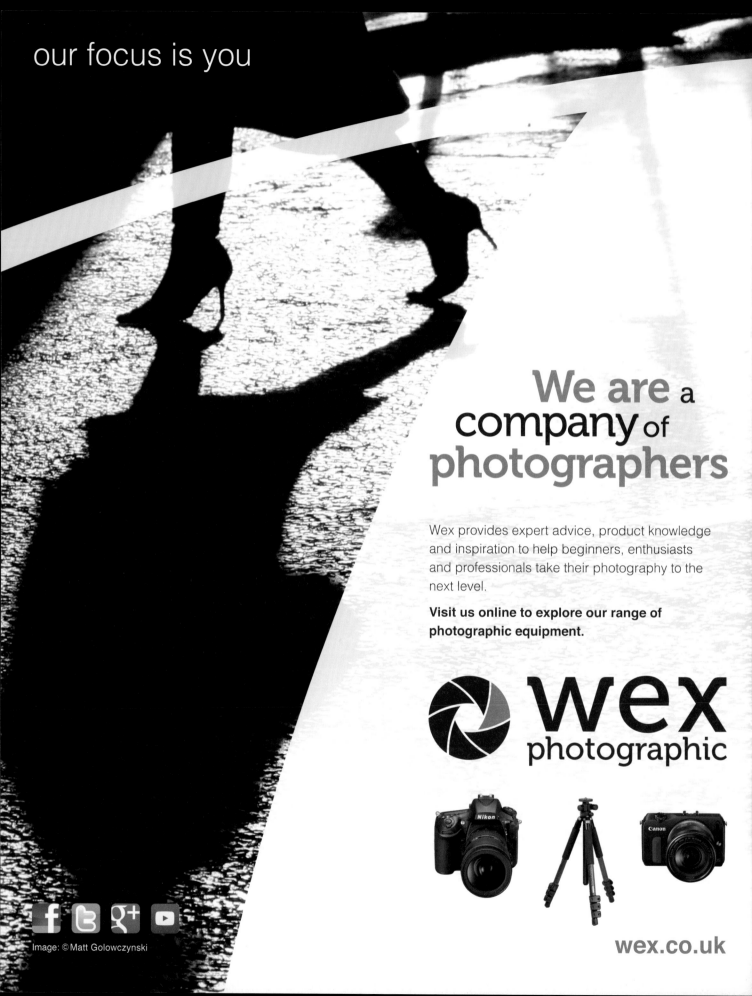

REBECOMING

THE OTHER EUROPEAN TRAVELLERS

CURATED BY TIM CLARK, 1000 WORDS

VIRGÍLIO FERREIRA

LUCY LEVENE

HENRIK MALMSTRÖM

TEREZA ZELENKOVA

AN EXHIBITION IN ASSOCIATION WITH
1000 WORDS AND FLOWERS GALLERY
EXHIBITION CLOSES 11 OCTOBER 2014

WWW.FLOWERSGALLERY.COM
WWW.1000WORDSMAG.COM

IMAGE: VIRGÍLIO FERREIRA, *BEING AND BECOMING* (DETAIL)

British Journal *of*
·PHOTOGRAPHY

SHOOT
AFTER
READING

The world's longest-running photography magazine,
now available for the iPad & iPhone.

GUP

042.

Guide to Unique Photography
Europe € 7,50
OPEN SPACE

GUP#42 OUT NOW

GUPMAGAZINE.COM

Photomonitor:

The webzine for photography in the UK & Ireland

Listings / Reviews / Interviews / Essays / Portfolio
Auctions / Collections / Books / Talks

www.photomonitor.co.uk

Rut Blees Luxemburg | *London Dust* | 2012 — As featured on *Photomonitor*

SOURCE DIGITAL EDITION

Available for iPad, iPhone or Android mobile devices

Four Issues per year
£4.99 per quarter
£17.99 Annual Subscription
10 back issues free for subscribers

from
www.exacteditions.com
www.source.ie/digitaledition

Or subscribe to the print edition at
www.source.ie

IPS Season of Photography 2015

The **Season of Photography** is a series of lively exhibitions and events taking place across Scotland from April to September 2015.

The **Institute for Photography in Scotland** (IPS) aims to enable awareness of and engagement with Scotland's photography, both nationally and internationally, and to promote collaboration amongst member bodies.

The IPS is an association between The National Galleries of Scotland, The University of Glasgow, The University of St Andrews, Street Level Photoworks, Glasgow, and Stills, Edinburgh.

Ponte City:
Mikhael Subotzky and Patrick Waterhouse
6 December 2014 to 26 April 2015

Lee Miller and Picasso
23 May to 6 September 2015

Bailey's Stardust
18 July to 18 October 2015

Document Scotland
Opens September 2015

NATIONAL GALLERIES SCOTLAND

nationalgalleries.org

Cyanotypes
by Anna Atkins and Anne Dixon
25 April to 12 July 2015

kennardphillipps
31 July to 18 October 2015

Stills

stills.org

Maud Sulter
25 April to 28th June 2015

Open for Business
9 Magnum Photographers
3 July to 6 September 2015

streetlevelphotoworks.org

·EDINBVRGH·
THE CITY OF EDINBURGH COUNCIL

Glasgow
CITY COUNCIL

CREATIVE SCOTLAND
ALBA | CHRUTHACHAIL

institutephotographyscotland.org

Get ahead in photography

IdeasTap is a charity that helps people get ahead in the creative industries.

We work with leading organisations – including **Magnum Photos**, **Metro Imaging**, **FORMAT Festival**, Photoworks, **Night Contact** and **Oxfam** – to help photographers develop and showcase their talent.

Our members have won prize money, project funding, industry mentoring, portfolio reviews, exhibition opportunities, and paid NGO commissions.

Join today for free at **www.ideastap.com/register**

"China: The Human Price of Pollution" Photo by Souvid Datta, winner of the 2013 IdeasTap Photographic Award with Magnum Photos.

THE INSTITUTE OF PHOTOGRAPHY

Photo © Beth Crutchfield

BA(Hons) Photography
BA(Hons) Press & Editorial Photography
BA(Hons) Marine & Natural History Photography
MFA

Tel: +44 (0)1326 213730
Email: admissions@falmouth.ac.uk

www.falmouth.ac.uk/photography-courses

FALMOUTH
UNIVERSITY

MK Gallery

Exhibition

An-My Lê

Admission free
19 September –
23 November 2014

This autumn MK Gallery presents the first major solo show in the UK by the Vietnamese-American photographer An-My Lê, including the most comprehensive showing to date of *Events Ashore* (2005-2014).

Above: An-My Lê: *US Naval Hospital Ship Mercy, Vietnam* (detail), 2009. From *Events Ashore* (2005-2014). Image courtesy of the artist and Murray Guy, New York.

Right: An-My Lê: *Small Wars, (Explosion)* (detail), 1999-2002. Image courtesy the artist and Murray Guy, New York.

MK Gallery is supported by:

Exhibition curated by Kate Bush
In partnership with:
Hasselblad Foundation, Gothenburg
MAS | Museum aan de Stroom, Antwerp
With thanks to: Murray Guy, New York

MK Gallery
900 Midsummer Blvd
Milton Keynes MK9 3QA
T +44 (0)1908 676 900
www.mkgallery.org

Middlesex
University
London

BA Photography
MA Photography

Our award-winning
courses based in
London have some of
the best facilities in
the country and world
class teaching staff
including Professor
Richard Billingham.

Look at some of the
work the students
have produced on
our website.

Come and see for
yourself on an
Open Day.

www.mdx.ac.uk

MA PHOTOGRAPHY AND URBAN CULTURES

Goldsmiths
UNIVERSITY OF LONDON

Now in its thirteenth year, this international programme explores cities through the lenses of photography, sociology, cultural geography, social anthropology and art history.

It will appeal to those whose visual and research practices ask questions about the politics and histories of contemporary urban life.

Course Leader: Paul Halliday

Programme Information:
http://www.gold.ac.uk/pg/ma-photography-urban-cultures/
Email: sociology.masters@gold.ac.uk

Photo / Stefano Carnelli

WESTMINSTER PHOTOGRAPHY

BA PHOTOGRAPHIC ARTS

BA PHOTOGRAPHY (4 YEARS PART TIME)

BA/BSC IMAGING ART & SCIENCE

MA PHOTOGRAPHIC STUDIES

MA PHOTOJOURNALISM & DOCUMENTARY PHOTOGRAPHY

PHD PROGRAMME

westminsterphotography.co.uk

UNIVERSITY OF
WESTMINSTER

Capture your creativity

One-off course or a
BA(Hons) Photography

Study at your own pace from home
and start at a time to suit you.

Support from a one to one tutor who
is also a practising photographer.

Be part of a UK and international
student community.

MA Fine Art online also available.
Find out more from our website.

Open College of the Arts

0800 731 2116
oca-uk.com

Eleanor Quinn OCA student

LEARN TO LOOK DEEPER

Discover Solent's practical, theory-driven photography courses

Find out more about our top-up, honours
and master's degrees at one of our open days

Your future's waiting
www.solent.ac.uk/opendays

Southampton
SOLENT
University

Photograph by Gunvor Eline Eng Jakobsen, student

rochester
UNDERGRADUATE – POSTGRADUATE – RESEARCH

BA (HONS) FASHION PHOTOGRAPHY
BA (HONS) PHOTOGRAPHY
MA PHOTOGRAPHY
MPHIL/PHD

OPEN DAYS 2014: Sat 27 Sep, Wed 15 Oct, Wed 29 Oct, Sat 15 Nov, Wed 3 Dec, 2015: Fri 9 Jan, Wed 25 Feb

For more information and to register on open days, please go to www.ucreative.ac.uk/opendays.

Please visit www.ucaphoto.com to view student work, and for course information please see:
www.ucreative.ac.uk/ba-fashion-photography
www.ucreative.ac.uk/ba-photography-rochester
www.ucreative.ac.uk/ma-photography
www.ucreative.ac.uk/research-degrees

MEDWAY
PHOTO
FESTIVAL

MEDWAY PHOTO FESTIVAL JANUARY 2015

MEDWAY PHOTO FESTIVAL celebrates its seventh edition in 2015. Exhibitions will feature exciting new work from students in their 2nd year studying BA (Hons) Photography and interim work from the MA Photography, alongside two Medway Fellowship projects, a School and Colleges Photo Competition and engaging events on photography. Since last year, the festival has become part of the RECREATE project for Medway, a project initiated in 2011. RECREATE is a network of organisations in France and England that share a common maritime border: the Channel. Selected under the European Cross-border Cooperation Programme INTERREG IVA France (Channel) England, co-funded by the ERDF, Recreate aims to encourage common citizenship and identity, and increase a sense of belonging to the cross-border area. Recreate concentrates on economic development and regeneration of urban town centres by transforming disused building into workspaces for the creative and cultural industries. Through a range of initiatives such as mentoring and networking, it aims establish and support individuals and small businesses from the creative industries. For more information about the Recreate project please see http://www.recreateproject.eu. For information on the fellowships and competitions please see www.ucaphoto.com. For the Medway Photo Festival please see www.medwayphoto.co.uk.

france mancha channel england
interreg

European Regional Development Fund
The European Union, investing in your future

Fonds européen de développement régional
L'Union européenne investit dans votre avenir

UCA
university for the **creative arts**

Photo: Ingrid Gustafsson

MA Photography

Located in the Northern Centre of Photography, our MA Photography offers you the opportunity to engage in a broad range of photographic practice. The course encourages the development of self-initiated project work, extending your technical, creative, intellectual and research skills. The staff team includes practicing artists, theorists, art curators and technical support, who together with visiting speakers and NEPN, support an exciting and current curriculum, providing new opportunities to enhance your practice.

Wanderer Above the Sea of Fog

Juliet Chenery-Robson

Farnham

BA (Hons) Photography
MFA Photography
Research Degrees

Photo: Jamie Carruthers BA (Hons) 2014 Graduate

View work by current students and graduates:
http://fotofolios.org/institution/universitycreativeartsfarnham
http://www.48degrees.co.uk/

Course information:
www.ucreative.ac.uk/ba-photography-farnham

Open days:
www.ucreative.ac.uk/opendays

Contact: 01252 892753
Course Leader: Joy Gregory

UCA
university for the creative arts

University of Brighton Photography

Supporting creativity, critical thinking, independence

BA (Hons) Photography   **MA Photography**   **BA (Hons) Moving Image**   **PhD**

Course tutors: Tim Brown, Stephen Bull, Jim Cooke, Denis Doran, Fergus Heron, Judith Katz, Joanna Lowry, Sally Miller, Matthew Noel-Tod, Mark Power, Judy Price, Xavier Ribas, Aaron Schuman, Julia Winckler

Recent visiting lecturers have included: Ignacio Acosta, Ed Atkins, Jonathan Baggaley, Lisa Barnard, Robert Beavers, Peter Bennett, Alison Bettles, Helen Cammock, Daniel Campbell Blight, Emma Charles, Emma Critchley, Nick Collins, Benedict Drew, Victoria Jenkins, Geert Van Kesteren, Kamila Kuc, Jo Longhurst, Gordon MacDonald, Yiorgos Nikiteas, Laure Prouvost, James Richards, Simon Roberts, Indre Serpytyte, Maria Short, Lindsey Smith, Stuart Smith, John Stezaker, Clare Strand, Danny Treacy

Photograph: The Draft by Matt Henry, MA Photography

University of Brighton   arts.brighton.ac.uk   samadmissions@brighton.ac.uk

ARCHIVAL PHOTOGRAPHIC
C-TYPE PRINTS AND EPSON
GICLÉE PRINTS

ARCHIVAL PRINT MOUNTING
AND FINISHING

DELIVERY SERVICE

SPONSORING
BRIGHTON PHOTO BIENNIAL 2014

SPECTRUM ▦

WWW.SPECTRUMPHOTO.CO.UK

01273 708222 | info@spectrumphoto.co.uk

constructing worlds

photography and architecture in the modern age

barbican

a journey through 20th
and 21st century architecture
by eighteen exceptional
international photographers

barbican.org.uk

**25 sep 2014—
11 jan 2015**

Media partner
Wallpaper*

Iwan Baan, *Torre David*, 2011
Image courtesy of the artist and Perry Rubenstein Gallery, Los Angeles

**CITY
OF
LONDON**

The City of London
Corporation is the founder
and principal funder
of the Barbican Centre

Cover image:
© Michael Rodgers and Nick Scammell

Back cover image:
© Michael Rodgers and Nick Scammell

Photoworks Annual
Published by Photoworks

photoworks

58-67 Grand Parade, Brighton, BN2 9QA, England, UK

t +44 (0)1273 643908
info@photoworks.org.uk
www.photoworks.org.uk
facebook.com/photoworksuk
twitter: @photoworks_uk

Editors:
Ben Burbridge and Celia Davies

Advertising & Distribution: Helen Wade, helen@photoworks.org.uk
Membership: Deborah Bullen, deborah@photoworks.org.uk www.photoworks.org.uk/members
Magazine Assistant: Alice Compton
Copy Editor: Rich Cutler

Photoworks team
Director: Celia Davies
Programme Curators: Ben Burbridge & Mariama Attah
General Manager: Deborah Bullen
Sales and Marketing Manager: Helen Wade
Learning & Participation Curator: Juliette Buss
Programme and Participation Coordinator: Alice Compton
Digital Designer & Developer: Kevin Beck
Education Coordinator: Claire Wearn
Volunteers: Sarah Dickenson, Isabella Smith, Amy Bartholomew, Jessica Gatfield, Alexandra Lethbridge

Art direction: David Lane
Design: David Lane & Lynne Devine

Printed in Holland by Lecturis
Printed on symbol tatami 135gsm, supplied by Fedrigoni Benelux

UK and European Distribution
Antenne Books: www.antennebooks.com
Contact: Bryony Lloyd, bryony@antennebooks.com

North American Distribution
Disticor Magazine Distribution Services: www.disticor.com
Contact: Carolyn Owens, carolyno@disticor.com

Photoworks is an organisation dedicated to enabling participation in photography, the most democratic medium of contemporary visual culture. Photoworks' programme includes commissions, publishing and participation. In collaboration with local, national and international partners, Photoworks connects outstanding artists with audiences and champions talent and ambition. Photoworks produces Brighton Photo Biennial, the UK's leading curated photography festival, promoting new thinking around photography through a commissioned programme of events and exhibitions.

Inside cover: Arrest of Pietro Valpreda,
Milan, 15 December, 1969.
© TEAM Editorial Services/Alinari

Inside back cover:
© Judy Harrison

Supported using public funding by